I am a companion of
and of them that
—Psalm 119:63

Words of Appreciation from Companions of Don Gossett

"As a new believer, two of my favorite teachers were E. W. Kenyon and Don Gossett. When I read their words the Holy Spirit bubbles within me. This *now* word was prepared three months before Don went to heaven. It is literally a word from heaven."

—*Sid Roth*
Host, *It's Supernatural!*

"Throughout the years, Don Gossett was such a great blessing to my family and ministry. The unconditional love from the Father that he consistently showed me aided in my restoration and recovery. Don never knew how much his personal example of humility, integrity, and devotion to the Lord means to me. He taught me so much."

—*Jim Bakker*
Host, *The Jim Bakker Show*

"We rejoice in God's goodness in giving Don Gossett to the church as a ministry gift over the years. I praise God for all Don's faithfulness. He blessed us here at *100 Huntley Street* every time he appeared as a guest. The viewers always responded favorably. On a personal level, Don was a huge encouragement to me."

—*David Mainse*
Founder and host, *100 Huntley Street*
Toronto, Canada

"I want to record what a blessing and encouragement Don's ministry was to the body of Christ in South Africa. The saints at Rhema send warm greetings and pray the Lord will continue to inspire and strengthen his ongoing ministry in the service of our soon-coming King."

—*Ray McCauley*
Rhema Bible Church
Randburg, South Africa

The following men of God, who have now passed on, each loved and worked with Don while here on this earth. Here are some excerpts from their personal correspondence with Don.

"What a wonderful testimony you have been to all those whom you have had contact with over the years. You have blessed so many. Only eternity will reveal how many lives you have touched and how many souls you have birthed into the kingdom of God as a result of your ministry and your giving heart."

—*Kenneth Hagin*
President, Kenneth Hagin Ministries

"I wanted to take this opportunity to express our gratitude for your faithfulness to God's calling on your life. Through the years you have made many sacrifices for the sake of the gospel and have walked through fires that many men would avoid. Only heaven will reveal the fruit of your obedience to the Master. You are a man whose unselfish love and friendship means a great deal to me."

—*T. L. Osborn*
Author and founder, Osborn Ministries International

"*The bush burned with fire, and the bush was not consumed*" (Exodus 3:2). We believe this characterizes your life. The bush is still burning and is not consumed! You have been able to accomplish in your life's span more than most people. Your achievements have been enviable. I applaud what the Lord has done through you. God blessed you for the many opportunities to expand God's great kingdom."

—*Paul Crouch*
President, Trinity Broadcasting Network

"In India and around the world, your ministry stands as a monument to God's greatness. How the people of India love our dear brother, Don Gossett."

—*Dr. D. G. S. Dhinakaran*
Founder and president, Jesus Calls Ministry
Chennai, India

"In the more than twenty years we have been friends, God has used you to touch my life. Sandra and I have sung in many countries around the world, but nothing moved us quite like ministering with you in India. We witnessed another side of Don Gossett, as you preached to the tens of thousands of people on the crusade grounds and then led them to salvation, healing, and deliverance. Brother Gossett, you stand head and shoulders above most men, and I want you to know that I admire and respect your life, your ministry, and your integrity as a true man of God. To God be the glory for the great things you have done."

—*Andraé* Crouch
Singer, songwriter, recording artist, pastor

"I will never forget the time that I ministered with you in a crusade in Trinidad. What a joy it was to get acquainted with you. May God's richest blessings be upon you, and may you have many more years of successful ministry."

—*R. W. Schambach*
Pastor, author, host of *Power Today*

"You have been a blessing to Whitaker House since 1973 through our personal contacts as well as through your many books. Your book, *What You Say Is What You Get*, was a bestseller in the United States and has been a blessing to me personally, as well as your other writings. You deserve an award for sticking with it all these years, through thick and thin. With a ministry as important as yours, I do hope you can continue to bless countless more readers by bringing them to a saving knowledge of our Lord and Savior Jesus Christ."

—*Robert Whitaker Sr.*
Founder and president, Whitaker House

FAITH
FOR
FINANCES

E. W. KENYON&
DON GOSSETT

WHITAKER
HOUSE

Unless otherwise indicated, all Scripture quotations are taken from the King James Version of the Holy Bible. Scripture quotations marked (ASV) are taken from the American Standard Edition of the Revised Version of the Holy Bible. Scripture quotations marked (WEY) are taken from *The New Testament in Modern Speech: An Idiomatic Translation into Everyday English from the Text of "The Resultant Greek Testament"* by R. F. (Richard Francis) Weymouth. Scripture quotations marked (RV) are taken from the Revised Version of the Holy Bible. Scripture quotations marked (YLT) are taken from Young's Literal Translation by Robert Young (1898).

Boldface type in the Scripture quotations indicates the author's emphasis.

Faith for Finances

www.kenyons.org
www.dongossett.com

ISBN: 978-1-62911-823-9
eBook ISBN: 978-1-62911-824-6
Printed in the United States of America
© 2017 by Debra Gossett

Whitaker House
1030 Hunt Valley Circle
New Kensington, PA 15068
www.whitakerhouse.com

Library of Congress Cataloging-in-Publication Data

Names: Kenyon, Essek William, 1867-1948, author.
Title: Faith for finances / by E.W. Kenyon and Don Gossett.
Description: New Kensington, PA : Whitaker House, 2017.
Identifiers: LCCN 2016049878 (print) | LCCN 2016051304 (ebook) | ISBN
   9781629118239 (trade pbk. : alk. paper) | ISBN 9781629118246 (E-book)
Subjects: LCSH: Success—Religious aspects—Christianity. | Success in
   business. | Finance, Personal—Religious aspects—Christianity.
Classification: LCC BV4598.3 .K47 2017 (print) | LCC BV4598.3 (ebook) | DDC
   248.4—dc23
LC record available at https://lccn.loc.gov/2016049878

1 2 3 4 5 6 7 8 9 10 11 LU 24 23 22 21 20 19 18 17

CONTENTS

INTRODUCTION: A WORD FROM DEBRA GOSSETT

Life-transforming influence can come in the form of a book. The small, handheld bonded papers can contain powerful seeds that explode in your heart and mind—destroying old, fruitless thinking and planting the potential of a whole new way of living. That's what happened to my late husband, Don Gossett.

Don received Jesus at the age of twelve, and in his late teens he answered a supernatural call to minister. At that time he had a bad stutter, but as he said "yes" to the Lord, God healed him and loosed his tongue to speak freely. Don hungrily embraced the Word of God early in his walk, and in those encounters, he began to understand that God and His Word are one. In his studies, he also discovered a book by E. W. Kenyon. Don's heart, and then his world, were set on fire. Next to the Bible, no works had a greater influence on Don than Kenyon's books. They satisfied his hunger like manna.

A few years later, Don heard about what the Lord was doing through T. L. Osborn, and he decided he would try to meet him face-to-face. He called the Osborn office in Tulsa, Oklahoma, to ask for an appointment to meet with Brother T. L. He was allotted thirty minutes. When Don arrived, the secretary said, "Good, you're on time. Please pay attention to the thirty-minute time limit. You may go in now." As Don entered T. L. Osborn's office he noticed a book by E. W. Kenyon lying on the desk. After their introductions and greetings, Don commented, "I see you read E. W. Kenyon." T. L. smiled and said enthusiastically, "Yes, E. W. Kenyon's writings have been my Bible School! And in fact, I travel overseas with copies of Kenyon's book *In His Presence* to give to any eager pastor I encounter." As they discussed the influence of Kenyon's writings, T. L. Osborn suddenly reached for his intercom and told his secretary, "Cancel all my appointments this afternoon. I want to fellowship more with this man."

A lifelong friendship was forged between T. L. Osborn and Don Gossett, and Don went to work for him for several years. Their lasting bond began with one book on a desk written by E. W. Kenyon.

Some years later Don moved from Tulsa to near Vancouver, Canada. When he heard that E. W. Kenyon's ministry office was near Seattle, he made an appointment to visit. There he met Ruth Kenyon, E. W. Kenyon's daughter, who was heading up the ministry. Ruth told Don that her father's writings were still in high demand all over the world.

"Ruth," Don asked, "how is it that your father had such revelation of God and His Word?"

"Oh, Don," she replied, "if you had lived in my home you would have seen my father with the open Bible constantly. One of my earliest and fondest childhood memories was walking by the sink where my dad was shaving. There, balanced on the sink ledge, was an open Bible. And there was my dad, with face lathered, the blade poised to shave, reading while tears made rivers through the cream on his face. He was smiling, weeping, and praising God for something he had just read."

Ruth's own heart was touched by the simple, direct truth of God's Word that Don conveyed. She read some items Don wrote and was impressed. Ruth expressed her respect for Don and how his belief in the Lord was like her father's. As their friendship developed, she mentioned that she had a box of unpublished material her father had written. After some time, Ruth gave Don the box of unfinished works and asked him to put them in print. She even suggested that Don incorporate them into his own books.

Instead of just quoting E. W. Kenyon in his books, Don combined his own writing with Kenyon's by alternating chapters. The first book written in this combined format of Don Gossett/E. W. Kenyon, the bestseller *The Power of Your Words*, was published exactly forty years ago,. This book is still one of the most popular books sent out by our ministry. Pastors have ordered it by the case for their congregations. Prisoners have written asking for a copy because they loaned it to a bunkmate who now wanted their own. The impact has been worldwide.

The power of God is released through revelation of His Word that we act upon in our lives. Throughout the years, when Don and I would travel and minister, we would take E. W. Kenyon's books with us to study as we prepared to bring the Good News of Jesus into nations such as India, Myanmar, Kenya, Papua New Guinea, UK, Australia, New Zealand, and more. Along with our Bibles, we would be refreshed and invigorated by E. W. Kenyon's *The Wonderful Name of Jesus*. Then we would go out and minister, whether to three people or to thousands, in His wonderful Name. The Lord healed and brought so many to salvation. Glory to God!

Several other E. W. Kenyon/Don Gossett books have since been published by our dear friends at Whitaker House. And a few months before Don passed away, he submitted a manuscript to our publisher. It was a book he had been discussing with me for years. He always wanted to write a book to help people "have faith for finances to live their lives and do what God called them to do." Here is that book!

Don penned his wish for you, the reader: *"I pray that these words will stir you to get the Word of God deep into your heart so that it will flow back out to change your world through the words you speak"* over your life's destiny, your finances, and your family. God wants you to have fulfillment in each of these vital areas. He is such a good, good God. Let's walk with Him and agree with Him. We give the Lord all the credit and glory for what He has done and is about to do!

This book you hold in your hands holds keys for your faith to be released for the Father's provision in your life. It is based on the living Word of our loving God. I pray you will meet with Him and discover freedom and *faith for finances* to help every aspect of your life!

—*Rev. Debra Gossett*
President, Don Gossett Ministries/Bold Bible Living
www.dongossett.com

PART I:
FAITH FOR FINANCIAL BLESSING

1

FAITH FOR FAMILY FINANCES

DON GOSSETT

As the provider for your family, I know how your honest spirit responds to the challenging words of 1 Timothy 5:8: *"But if any provide not for his own, and specially for those of his own house, he hath denied the faith, and is worse than an infidel."*

For the first eleven years that I was the provider for the Gossett family, I experienced continual financial hardships and difficulties. Becoming the proud and happy father of five children by the time I was twenty-eight years old compounded my problems, of course, for there were unrelenting financial requirements. Inability to meet my commitments on time produced embarrassment often. Those unexpected expenditures labeled "emergency" drained my resources and kept my back against the wall.

In October 1961, we were living in the beautiful island city of Victoria, British Columbia. Our financial situation was so deplorable, however, that it was hardly a pleasant experience. But something happened that month that changed our financial picture.

It was an all-night prayer meeting that changed everything for us. My first wife, Joyce, and I poured out our hearts to God. Perhaps I shall never forget her prayers that night. I had never heard anyone talk so frankly to our heavenly Father. It wasn't just a nagging, complaining series of utterances either. As we concluded that night of prayer, we were confident that our needs would always be met from that day onward. And they were, praise God!

God gave me a "secret" of faith for family finances that has never failed. He gave me my "Never Again" list as the foundation for a total change in my life.[1] Point number 2 on that list: Never again will I confess lack, for *"my God shall supply all* [my] *need according to his riches in glory by Christ Jesus"* (Philippians 4:19). The Lord revealed to me how I had limited Him in ministering to my needs because I constantly talked about my lack of money, my unpaid bills, and so forth. God asked me from Amos 3:3, *"Can two walk together, except they be agreed?"* I couldn't walk with God in financial supply if I disagreed with Him.

How was I disagreeing with God? By disagreeing with His Word. This Word of God became my new testimony. I agreed with God; I disagreed with the devil, who was keeping his oppressive hands on the finances. Never again have I been victimized by lack of money for my family.

There are principles I have learned that are God's Word. God honors hard, diligent work. Labor is usually God's way to meet needs. Often God has met my needs by my writings. Writing is hard work. Sitting up all night on a train to deliver a manuscript to a publisher is also tedious. But even more rewarding than the financial returns are the thousands of lives transformed by words I have written under the inspiring leadership of the Holy Spirit.

Not just work, but faith. Your faith is detectible by your words. Second Corinthians 4:13 says, *"We having the same spirit of faith, according as it is written, I believed, and therefore have I spoken; we also believe, and therefore speak."* Faith is released or expressed by your mouth.

---

1. The entire "Never Again" list can be found in *His Word Is Now* by E. W. Kenyon and Don Gossett, Whitaker House, 2016.

Speak your faith. That is, speak the Word.

Say often, "My God shall supply all my need." (See Philippians 4:19.) Those are seven words that will put you over the top, even as they have put me over financially. God absolutely watches over His Word to perform it.

There is no doubt about it: what you say is what you get. Speak of your lack of money, of how hard things are going for you, and you will get what you say. I urge you to confess often: "I have faith for finances for my family! Thank You, Father, for they are riches now." With your palms open, reach out to your Father and receive from Him.

2

OUT OF POVERTY INTO ABUNDANCE

DON GOSSETT

Speak the following seven declarations of abundance over your life.

1. Poverty is not God's will for my life. He says, *"Beloved, I wish above all things that thou mayest prosper and be in health, even as thy soul prospereth"* (3 John 2). Here and now I confess that I am through with poverty. The words *insufficiency* and *inadequacy* are no longer a part of my vocabulary.

2. Jesus came to give me *"life, and that…more abundantly"* (John 10:10). This abundant life of Christ overflows in physical and material abundance. In Jesus, abundance is mine!

3. The good news Jesus announced in Luke 4:18–19 included liberation from poverty. Never again shall I confess lack, for *"my God shall supply all [my] need according to his riches in glory by Christ Jesus"* (Philippians 4:19).

4. God is not poverty-stricken, and He doesn't produce poverty-stricken children. The Bible abounds with promises that God will open the windows of heaven, satisfy us, shower down on us, rain on us, pour into us, provide for us, replenish us, and prosper us.

5. The Bible clearly reveals that Satan is the devourer, the thief, and the destroyer. He seeks to consume our resources, deplete our money, and exhaust our financial ability. Not ignorant of his devices, I will *"resist the devil, and he will flee from* [me]" (James 4:7).

6. God promises that when I honor Him with my substance by giving Him the firstfruits of all my increase my reward shall be plenty. (See Proverbs 3:9–10.) "Plenty" means sufficient income, enough money, and satisfaction. When I pay my tithe (the first dime of every dollar, the first dollar of each ten) and give offerings above the tithe, God promises to deliver me from a hand-to-mouth existence and to prosper my way. (See Malachi 3:10.)

7. Poverty produces embarrassment. Distressing, difficult days are experienced when impoverished. No longer! I am *confessing* and *giving* my way to abundance, the place where God supplies all my needs. I now have the means to provide adequately for my family. I am in command of money instead of money in command of me. I give cheerfully, liberally, to my Lord. He gives back to me *"good measure, pressed down, and shaken together, and running over"* (Luke 6:38). Good bye, poverty. Thank You, God, for abundance!

3

STEPPING OUT

E. W. KENYON

Stepping out of sin-consciousness into Son-consciousness is stepping out of failure into success. It means stepping out of that inferiority complex that has held you prisoner for years. It means becoming the person you have dreamed of.

Perhaps you've heard the story of the little scrawny fellow who sat beside a great big, muscular man. When the strong man took his girl away from him, he went to the gymnasium to develop his muscles and become strong. Then he went out and faced the other man unafraid.

When you go into God's gymnasium, you come in contact with the great spiritual gymnastic Teacher. You let Him put you through a course until you can stand in front of the world complete in all His finished work, until your inferiority has been swallowed up in His dominant victorious Spirit, until you can whisper, "Greater is He who is in me than he who is in the world" or "Greater is He who is in me than the doubts and fears that worked in me in the past."

I have a Master now who builds me up instead of keeping me in bondage. I walked in failure for years. I walked with the sense of my lack of ability and righteousness; but now I walk with God. We are linked together. I am breathing in the courage of His tremendous personality. I am filled with His ability.

I said good-bye to the dark, unhappy days of the past. A curtain fell between them and me. I stand upon the highlands a victor.

No longer do I worry about the lack of money. Lack of money does not lord itself over me, either. I am master. Lack of ability does not lord itself over me now. Lack of opportunity no longer lords itself over me. I am not intimidated by circumstances or filled with fear that I cannot do the work or put it over. I know that the Mighty One has taken over me and has put me over since I stepped out of sin-consciousness and into Son-consciousness.

4

FINANCIAL PROSPERITY

DON GOSSETT

Freedom from financial worries is assured by God's Word. Many people are robbed of peace and joy in the Lord because of their constant worry about finances. As a Christian, however, if you are faithful in your tithes and offerings, you can claim the promises I share now. Banks may close and money may be devalued, but God's Word is sure forever.

1. *"Cast thy bread upon the waters: for thou shalt find it after many days"* (Ecclesiastes 11:1). This means that as you give unto the Lord, it will be given back to you in spiritual blessings, financial rewards, and eternal fruit to your account in heaven.

2. *"But rather seek ye the kingdom of God; and all these things shall be added unto you"* (Luke 12:31). Jesus was speaking about *"all these things"*—food, raiment, shelter—all these will be provided as you put Him first in your life and seek first the kingdom of God.

3. *"If then God so clothe the grass, which is to day in the field, and tomorrow is cast into the oven; how much more will he clothe you?"* (Luke 12:28). God's care for your life is

obvious, do not resist His generosity by worrying over material things.

4. *"But lay up for yourselves treasures in heaven, where neither moth nor rust doth corrupt, and where thieves do not break through nor steal"* (Matthew 6:20). The great assurance of investing your money in the Lord's service now is that it is treasure laid up in heaven to your account.

It is no sin to be poor; it's just mighty inconvenient. The Lord wants to prosper your life, to supply your own needs, and to enable you to give liberally and generously to spreading the gospel. It's the *love* of money that's the root of all evil. Ask God to give you the "gift of giving."

Your life will be immensely joyful as you live by this principle: "I live to give."

And this: "Life is to give and not to take."

5

THE JOY OF GIVING

DON GOSSETT

The most joyful Christians I have ever known are those who know the blessing of giving. They respond to God's Word, and God does what He says He will do:

> I am the LORD, I change not…. Bring ye all the tithes into the storehouse…and prove me now herewith, saith the LORD of hosts, if I will not open you the windows of heaven, and pour you out a blessing, that there shall not be room enough to receive it. And I will rebuke the devourer for your sakes.
> (Malachi 3:6, 10–11)

> Honour the LORD with thy substance, and with the firstfruits of all thine increase: so shall thy barns be filled with plenty.
> (Proverbs 3:9–10)

Through the years, my family has faced perilous situations more than once. Shortly after our daughter, Jeanne, was born with clubfoot, my wife was afflicted with rheumatic fever that threatened her life, and I had to leave the evangelistic field to care for my family. With no source of income, things became very discouraging.

In our desperate search for God's help, we discovered 2 Corinthians 9:6:

But this I say, He which soweth sparingly shall reap also sparingly; and he which soweth bountifully shall reap also bountifully.

If we sow bountifully of our limited means, God will enable us to reap bountifully. This act of faith was the spark plug that ignited all our faith actions, and we reaped mighty miracles of healing for both my wife and daughter, as well as financial blessings to provide for our family. I was even able to return to the Lord's calling of full-time ministry.

Romans 12:8 reveals that one of the gifts of the Holy Spirit is the gift of giving. Ask God for this gift in your life. God will prosper you so that you will be enabled to give generously to His great work.

And, when you give, boldly affirm these seven facts:

1. Even as I honor the Lord by seeking Him first (see Matthew 6:33); giving Christ the preeminence in all things (see Colossians 1:18); praising and worshiping Him; and praying and sharing my testimony, so I honor Him with my substance, even my financial increase.

2. As the wise men came from the East to honor the holy Child, Jesus, with gifts of gold, frankincense, and myrrh, so as a wise Christian, I honor Jesus with each gift for the spreading of His gospel.

3. When I give, I am not honoring the pastor, the church, the evangelist, the missionary, or this or that cause. My giving actually honors the Lord Jesus Christ! Honor my Lord—think of it! It removes the sense of rigid duty out of my giving and injects royal dignity and tribute to my King! Hallelujah, what a sweet privilege!

4. *"Then the people rejoiced, for that they offered willingly, because with perfect heart they offered willingly to the* LORD: *and David the king also rejoiced with great joy"* (1 Chronicles 29:9). I, too, am a willing giver, rejoicing with great joy.

5. *"Let us be glad and rejoice, and give honour to him"* (Revelation 19:7), even when we give each dollar unto the advancing of His gospel. The money I spend on myself, or on other things, perishes with the using; but the money I give to the Lord is treasure laid up in heaven (see Matthew 6:20), and I will never regret having given it, no, not in a million years from now!

6. Every time I give, I know I honor not man, church, or organization but the blessed Lord Himself! God says, *"Them that honour me I will honour"* (1 Samuel 2:30).

Through liberality in giving, you can experience immense joy. Meditate upon the following dynamic words of God:

Inasmuch as ye have done it unto one of the least of these my brethren, ye have done it unto me.   (Matthew 25:40)

Whosoever shall give you a cup of water to drink in my name, because ye belong to Christ, verily I say unto you, he shall not lose his reward.   (Mark 9:41)

He that giveth unto the poor shall not lack.
                                        (Proverbs 28:27)

If thou draw out thy soul to the hungry, and satisfy the afflicted soul; then shall thy light rise in obscurity, and thy darkness be as the noon day.   (Isaiah 58:10)

Bring ye all the tithes into the storehouse, that there may be meat in mine house, and prove me now herewith, saith the LORD of hosts, if I will not open you the windows of heaven, and pour you out a blessing, that there shall not be room enough to receive it. (Malachi 3:10)

The liberal soul shall be made fat [prosperous]: and he that watereth shall be watered also himself. (Proverbs 11:25)

He which soweth sparingly shall reap also sparingly; and he which soweth bountifully shall reap also bountifully. (2 Corinthians 9:6)

Blessed are the merciful: for they shall obtain mercy. (Matthew 5:7)

Every man according as he purposeth in his heart, so let him give; not grudgingly, or of necessity: for God loveth a cheerful giver. (2 Corinthians 9:7)

Be ye strong therefore, and let not your hands be weak: for your work shall be rewarded. (2 Chronicles 15:7)

Blessed is he that considereth the poor: the LORD will deliver him in time of trouble. (Psalm 41:1)

God is able to make all grace abound toward you; that ye, always having all sufficiency in all things, may abound to every good work. (2 Corinthians 9:8)

He that hath pity upon the poor lendeth unto the LORD; and that which he hath given will he pay him again. (Proverbs 19:17)

Give, and it shall be given unto you; good measure, pressed down, and shaken together, and running over, shall men give into your bosom. For with the same measure that ye mete withal it shall be measured to you again.   (Luke 6:38)

You now know that God promises you prosperity and plenty because you are liberal in giving unto Him. This makes your giving a noble privilege! Have you praised Him for enabling you to give?

6

DEVELOP YOUR RESOURCES

E. W. KENYON

Most of us are like wild land—undeveloped. We show signs of real wealth, but it lies underneath roots and stumps, and we refuse to clear the land and make the soil usable.

Here is a voice with marvelous timbre but no training. They write across it "Unusable/Undeveloped." Here is a face with a smile but no fortune, because the mind is untrained, unfit, and unready. We write across it "Unavailable."

What we need is hard work—not work on impulse but on principle. We need to drive ourselves until we have developed the rich resources within us.

And the time to do it is now. Begin today to clean up that rich bottom land in your nature, and get it into production at once. Make everything swing into line with the one great objective of your life. Determine your future, settle what you are going to do, and then make every day pay tribute. Form habits of study, habits of industry. Learn to save the moments; the hours will take care of themselves. Form the habit of concentration—downright hard thinking. Drive your mind. Become an absolute slave driver of your own faculties. They are your slaves, your servants. Make them work. Make them study. Make them develop.

Kill laziness and that draining habit of dreaming. Transform it into vital energy. Set the dynamo of a tremendous purpose loose inside of you. Indecision and wastefulness of ability and time must be destroyed. Fight for time. It is the most valuable asset you have. Cut every corner. Save every moment. Be exact with yourself. Put yourself on a schedule. Make yourself do your best. Wasting time is wasting ability. It is wasting the thing that makes you worthwhile. Learn to use it. Make your time your wealth. Make moments pay dividends. Carve success for tomorrow out of every day.

Make yourself worthwhile. Make people want you. Make yourself so attractive, so valuable, that men will hunt after you.

Make opportunities where no opportunities existed before. Then make yourself ready for the opportunity.

7

HOW TO GET A BETTER JOB

DON GOSSETT

1. *"Seek not ye what ye shall eat, or what ye shall drink, neither be ye of doubtful mind. For all these things do the nations of the world seek after: and your Father knoweth that ye have need of these things"* (Luke 12:29–30). Your Father knows that you need a better job to better provide for your family and to give more generously to help spread the gospel. He knows whether your working conditions in your present employment are suitable. The phrase *"Neither be ye of doubtful mind"* is highly essential in receiving from the Lord a better job. Doubt about God providing will close the door to better employment. Doubt is of the devil and is the pathway to defeat.

2. *"Delight thyself also in the LORD: and he shall give thee the desires of thine heart"* (Psalm 37:4). Perhaps the desire of your heart is to have a better job. Then delight yourself in the Lord by pleasing Him and praising Him.

3. *"Every one that asketh receiveth; and he that seeketh findeth; and to him that knocketh it shall be opened"* (Matthew 7:8). Make this your prayer: "My heavenly Father, I ask

You in Jesus' name to provide me a better job. You know why I need a better job, and I thank You for providing for my need. In Jesus' name, amen."

4. *"As long as he sought the* LORD, *God made him to prosper"* (2 Chronicles 26:5). This is a key to prosperity: Take time to seek the Lord by prayer, study His Word, and honor Him in your giving.

5. *"Your heavenly Father knoweth that ye have need of all these things"* (Matthew 6:32). *"[Cast] all your care upon him; for he careth for you"* (1 Peter 5:7). With total assurance, cast your need for a better job upon the Lord, who cares so much for you.

6. *"The* LORD *God is a sun and shield: the* LORD *will give grace and glory: no good thing will he withhold from them that walk uprightly"* (Psalm 84:11). Because you walk uprightly before Him, He will not withhold any *"good thing"*—your new and better job!

8

EXCELLENT RECEIVERS

DON GOSSETT

God promises us that He will supply all your needs in Christ (see Philippians 4:19), but Christians don't always know how to receive His provision. The following points are to help you excellently receive all that God has for you.

1. Many people are "expert askers" but not so successful in receiving from God. Jesus said, *"Ask, and ye shall receive"* (John 16:24). But not only ask but also boldly expect to receive! After we ask the Father, we should begin to expect the answer. We should begin to praise the Lord in faith for the answer, even before we have seen or felt the evidence.

2. We must not hinder receiving by having any wrong spirit. Jesus said, *"When ye stand praying, forgive, if ye have ought against any"* (Mark 11:25). These following things will hinder our receiving answers to prayer: unforgiveness, hidden resentments, covered-up malice, and ill-will. Spiritual power cannot flow through our lives with unforgiveness and resentment. Ask the Lord to take away all grudges, hate, and jealousy.

3. Again, Jesus said, *"Love your enemies, bless them that curse you, do good to them that hate you, and pray for them which despitefully use you, and persecute you"* (Matthew 5:44). Do not go to the level of your enemies and hate. Seek no retaliation. Make a list of the people who have hurt or mistreated you, and pray for each one by name. Practice forgiving them. Don't seek justification in your resentment. Learn to speak kindly of these people. The effect upon your own Christian life will be amazing, and will oftentimes break down barriers. Keep the channel of your own heart clear and clean, so that the Spirit can flow through you.

4. *"My God shall supply all your need according to his riches in glory by Christ Jesus"* (Philippians 4:19). This power-house Scripture means exactly what it says it means— all your needs are met in Christ Jesus. As revealed in the Word, you will discover the supply of every need in your life through Christ. Ask Him to meet every specific need. Then confess it all is yours, *"according to his riches in glory by Christ Jesus."* But don't ask Him for something today and then come back tomorrow and ask for the same thing in an unbelieving manner. In doing so, you annul your prayer for today.

5. Praise is the golden key for appropriating all your need from the Father's supply. He has promised, you have asked Him to do it, so act as if He is doing it by praising Him!

9

USING WHAT IS IN YOU

E. W. KENYON

There is a gold mine hidden in every life. Nature has never made a failure. Every man has success hidden away in his soul, but no one can find it but himself. He holds the key to the hidden room.

Failure comes because we never seek that hidden treasure. Failure comes because we try to find it somewhere else. You can't find it anywhere else.

Success, victory, and achievement are in you. Exceptional people are those who develop what is within them.

That quartet is winning fame and success because they developed what they had in them. Singly they could not do it, but united they make a harmony that thrills the heart.

I have seen great soloists do this. Talent is in them, and they developed it and made it of commercial value.

I have seen three great baritones. One was a miner who, had he not been too lazy and loved the companionship of drinking men and useless women, would have been known the world over. What a voice he had. I picked him up a drunkard. I tried to make a man of him. I bought him clothes. However, when it was known that Scotty was going to sing, the building could not hold the crowd.

I said to him, "I don't know whether my pianist can play the pieces that you want to sing without looking them over." He looked at me with a peculiar expression and said, "I need no accompaniment."

He stood by the piano in his old mining clothes one night and sang. I closed my eyes but couldn't locate him, because his voice utterly filled that whole room. He seemed to be everywhere in it. That great voice made strange, sweet, wonderful music. He remade all the songs he sang that night.

I raised money and sent him back to his own land. He promised to sing again. As a boy, Scotty sang in Drewry but confessed that he had been so drunk that another man had to hold him up. He never amounted to anything. He did not develop the thing that was in him.

Some people waste genius because they do not develop it. I know it is hard work, but you will learn to love hard work. There are no great gold nuggets lying on top of the earth. You have to go down into the earth for them; you must dig for them.

You want the applause of the world? You want money to buy fine clothes and build splendid houses? Awaken, young men. Go find that hidden place in your own nature. Dig and dig until you have conquered.

A father was dying. He had two sons. The boys had always thought that he had gold hidden away somewhere. He had never been a strong, healthy man, so his ten acres of stump land had never been developed. When he was dying, he called it "the stump lot." Again and again, he said, "the stump lot."

As soon as the funeral was over, the boys said, "The gold is out in the stump lot." How feverishly they worked to find it. They tore up every inch of it, but they found no gold. Then the older one said, "We have the land in good condition, let's put in corn." In the autumn, they found gold in the ripened corn.

You have a stump lot in you. Dig it up, clean it up, and you will find gold in it.

10

STOP WORRYING ABOUT FINANCES

DON GOSSETT

Worry about money problems? How often I've experienced this worry. Has financial worry ever robbed you of your Son of joy? God's Word assures us of freedom from financial worries. Many people are robbed of peace and joy in the Lord because of their constant worry about finances. As a Christian, however, if you are faithful in your tithes and offerings, you can claim the promises I share now. Banks may close and money may be devaluated, but God's Word is sure forever.

Read the following reasons why you need never worry again about finances.

1. *"My God shall supply all your need according to his riches in glory by Christ Jesus"* (Philippians 4:19).

2. "Keep on asking and you will keep on getting; keep on looking and you will keep on finding; knock, and the door will be opened." (See Luke 11:9.)

3. *"Consider the ravens: for they neither sow nor reap; which neither have storehouse nor barn; and God feedeth them:*

how much more are ye better than the fowls?" (Luke 12:24).

4. "[Cast] all your care upon him; for he careth for you" (1 Peter 5:7).

5. "The LORD will give grace and glory: no good thing will he withhold from them that walk uprightly" (Psalm 84:11).

6. "Your heavenly Father knoweth that ye have need of all these things" (Matthew 6:32).

7. "Hitherto have ye asked nothing in my name: ask, and ye shall receive, that your joy may be full" (John 16:24).

8. "Fear not, little flock; for it is your Father's good pleasure to give you the kingdom" (Luke 12:32).

9. "Trust in the LORD, and do good; so shalt thou dwell in the land, and verily thou shalt be fed" (Psalm 37:3).

10. "I have been young, and now am old; yet have I not seen the righteous forsaken, nor his seed begging bread" (Psalm 37:25).

11. "If ye then, being evil, know how to give good gifts unto your children, how much more shall your Father which is in heaven give good things to them that ask him?" (Matthew 7:11).

12. "But rather seek ye the kingdom of God; and all these things shall be added unto you" (Luke 12:31). "All these things"—food, raiment, shelter—that Jesus was speaking about will be provided as you put Him first in your life and seek first His kingdom.

13. "A little that a righteous man hath is better than the riches of many wicked" (Psalm 37:16).

14. "Even the very hairs of your head are all numbered. Fear not therefore: ye are of more value than many sparrows" (Luke 12:7).

15. *"If then God so clothe the grass, which is to day in the field, and to morrow is cast into the oven; how much more will he clothe you…?"* (Luke 12:28).

16. *"Your Father knoweth that ye have need of these things"* (Luke 12:30).

17. *"Cast thy bread upon the waters: for thou shalt find it after many days"* (Ecclesiastes 11:1). This means that as you give unto the Lord, it will be given back to you in spiritual blessings, financial reward, and eternal fruit.

18. *"But lay up for yourselves treasures in heaven, where neither moth nor rust doth corrupt, and where thieves do not break through nor steal"* (Matthew 6:20). The great assurance of investing your money in the Lord's service is that it is treasure laid up in your account in heaven.

As we live by John 3:16 with assurance of salvation, we can also live by these blessed verses for provision of every financial need. Expect daily fulfillment of these words of God as long as you live! Praise Him!

11

THE MENTAL HITCHHIKER

E. W. KENYON

Are fish worth the cost of the pole, line, and hooks? Are honor and competence in old age worth saving, self-denial, and hard work in youth? Would it not be better to spend your money and squander your time knowing that when old age comes, there will be a monthly pension?

These are questions that face earnest young people today. We can spend our time in the roadhouse, in shows or dances, or idly roaming the streets; or we can drive ourselves to study and fit ourselves for the place that is waiting.

Everywhere big businesses are hunting for competent help. Many mediocre men fill places of importance because no one can find people who are really fitted for the job. It is surprising how difficult it is to find even a good stenographer or someone who can take charge of a department and make it a success or someone who will take a vital interest in his work and excel in it.

Every man and woman is a "time server." Everyone's ambition is to get his wages with as little work as possible. The new mental attitude is to get without giving. But you cannot be a success and do that.

The good old days of honest labor seem to be but a dream today. The road that leads to a good bank account is an uphill road, and most of us have to build the road ourselves.

Hitchhikers are filling the road today. They want someone else's car to ride in. They want someone to buy the gas. They want someone to pay the taxes and give them free passage.

Are you a mental hitchhiker? Are you a mental hobo? Or are you one of the fellows who pays his taxes, builds the roads, and bears the burdens?

If you want to be a success, you will have to bear the burdens. You will have to pay the taxes for a hundred other people. The easy way is to hobo it. It is the way of least resistance.

I believe a fellow can get used to living on short rations, wearing old clothes, and sleeping in the jungle; but as for me, I am going to get to the top.

I am sending out this invitation for the rest of you to come with me.

12

THE GIVER'S CREED

DON GOSSETT

1. I live to give, for I *"remember the words of the Lord Jesus, how he said, It is more blessed to give than to receive"* (Acts 20:35).

2. I live to give cheerfully unto the Lord. *"Every man according as he purposeth in his heart, so let him give; not grudgingly, or of necessity: for God loveth a cheerful giver"* (2 Corinthians 9:7).

3. I live to give according to the measure of the blessing of the Lord I have received. *"Every man shall give as he is able, according to the blessing of the LORD thy God which he hath given thee"* (Deuteronomy 16:17).

4. I live to give, for this is the way of love. *"God so loved the world, that he gave his only begotten Son"* (John 3:16). Christ Jesus *"loved me, and gave himself for me"* (Galatians 2:20).

5. I live to give tithes and offerings. The results are evident—open windows in heaven, overflowing blessings there's not room enough to contain, the rebuke of Satan

for my sake, plus other benefits. I affirm with Jacob, *"Of all that thou shalt give me I will surely give the tenth unto thee"* (Genesis 28:22).

6. I live to give freely because the Lord has given so much to me. *"Freely [I] have received, freely [I] give"* (Matthew 10:8).

7. I live to give, for giving is the essence of living. I *"give, and it shall be given unto* [me]; *good measure, pressed down, and shaken together, and running over, shall men give into* [my] *bosom. For with the same measure that* [I] *mete withal it shall be measured to* [me] *again"* (Luke 6:38).

8. I live to give, for this is the life of sowing and reaping. *"But this I say, He which soweth sparingly shall reap also sparingly; and he which soweth bountifully shall reap also bountifully"* (2 Corinthians 9:6).

9. When I live by this creed—"I live to give"—I will never live in lack. When I live to give my money away, God sees to it that I always have enough for my needs and, even more important, for His purposes for me.

13

UNANSWERED PRAYERS

DON GOSSETT

"I have caught the vision, and for self I cannot live; life is less than worthless till my all I give."
—*Oswald J. Smith*

The most important thing a person can do with money is give it away. How sweet is the life of giving! The promises of God on giving are so definite. The Bible says, *"It is more blessed to give than to receive"* (Acts 20:35).

So what about the person who doesn't give? What can he expect? For one, his prayers may not be answered.

If your prayers are not being answered, you should take stock on the matter of your giving. God has a divine law of giving and receiving. In the measure that you give, so shall you receive from God. If you rob God in giving, you are the loser in the long run.

Because I love you and am zealous for God's best for you, I urge you: Don't go on with the firm disapproval of God upon your life. Give unto the Lord. In this day of Holy Spirit renewal and great need of the gospel, there has never been a greater time for generous, bountiful givers in the name of the Lord. God will do what He has promised long ago in response to generous giving— He will open the windows of heaven, pour out overflowing blessings, and rebuke the devourer for your sake. (See Malachi 3:11.)

Are you stingy with God, and therefore dry, barren, and empty? If so, you are paying for your disobedience in spiritual leanness.

A man once asked me, "Do you mean I have to buy the blessing of God by giving my money?" I replied, "Absolutely not. You can't buy anything from God. But when you cheerfully, liberally give, you honor strong commands. You are cooperating with your Creator. Therefore, you can be sure that God will do exactly what He said."

The Bible says that withholding from God tends to lead to poverty. On the contrary, giving to the Lord tends to produce tremendous spiritual, physical, and financial blessings. Thousands of people testify to this fact.

If you are having financial worries, try God's methods of giving, and then receive His bounties. The life of giving is a beautiful life.

14

THE BELL RINGER

E. W. KENYON

Selling from house to house is a good place to start life. You meet a different person every five minutes, and if you can get them to listen to you, you have a foot in the door. So many simply will say, "I haven't time," and then slam the door in your face. You will have to smile and go to the next. That's the game.

But the man who can get inside the house to display his goods is the man who puts it over. The first requisite is a smile—not an ingratiating smile but a wholesome, big, warm smile—and a glad "Good morning." To be successful, you must know that you have something that they need, something they ought to have. You should come there with the heart of a philanthropist, because you have something to give. They are going to get something worth more than they pay for it. Therefore, you are not trying to outdo them; you are there to give them something worthwhile.

I didn't know anything about the sales game when I went into it as a boy of twenty-one. Salesmanship was not taught then as it is today. I became one of the pioneers of sales talk, teaching the art of salesmanship. But I found that I could not sell unless I had confidence in the thing I was selling.

At one point, I was selling pianos and organs from house to house. I tried to sell instruments in which I had no confidence, and I was an utter failure.

One day, I went back to the office and asked the manager what was the best piano for such a price. He told me. I went to the factory to find out all about pianos, because I wanted to know how the things were built. I studied them until I knew everything a young fellow could learn about the instruments. Then I went out on the road.

I knew that I had the best thing on the market for the money. I knew that if I could get a piano into a house, and have the boys and girls practice on it, it would change the future of that home. I went out to help the community, and I succeeded. It was so easy to sell when I had the right mental attitude toward the people. I was trying to bless and help my clients.

Do you see the point? That is the real art of salesmanship. I was so dead in earnest about it. I was so enthusiastic about the bargain I had that I carried them off their feet. I sold to people who had no music in them. I sold to them because of the excessive, burning desire in my heart to make them happy. That is what sells.

Settle it in your own mind. Is the thing you are selling worthwhile? If it is not, then get something that is.

If you are selling insurance, bonds, autos, or groceries, know this: If your entire ambition is simply to get the money out of it, you will fail. But if you are giving them something that is going to be a blessing, and you are enthusiastic over it, you will be a success.

15

THE ONE WHO MAKES GIVING POSSIBLE

DON GOSSETT

Consider first of all that the Lord is your Creator and everything you have to give is made possible because of His giving to you. *"The earth is the Lord's, and the fulness thereof"* (1 Corinthians 10:26). This Scripture is quoted several times in both the Old and New Testaments. Again the Lord says, *"The silver is mine, and the gold is mine, saith the LORD of hosts"* (Haggai 2:8). In addition, God rightfully claims all creatures:

> For every beast of the forest is mine, and the cattle upon a thousand hills. I know all the fowls of the mountains: and the wild beasts of the field are mine. If I were hungry, I would not tell thee: for the world is mine, and the fulness thereof.
> (Psalm 50:10–12)

Further proof that the Lord is the One who makes it possible for you to give is in John's statement *"A man can receive nothing, except it be given him from heaven"* (John 3:27). Paul asks, *"What hast thou that thou didst not receive?"* (1 Corinthians 4:7). If you are profitable in your work, have you considered the Source?

Thus saith the LORD, *thy Redeemer, the Holy One of Israel;
I am the* LORD *thy God which teacheth thee to profit, which
leadeth thee by the way that thou shouldest go.*

(Isaiah 48:17)

It is God Himself who gives you the power to get material
things.

It is [God] *that giveth thee power to get wealth.*

(Deuteronomy 8:18)

The Bible makes it very clear that riches and honor come from
the Lord.

*Both riches and honour come of thee, and thou reignest over
all; and in thine hand is power and might; and in thine hand
it is to make great, and to give strength unto all. Now therefore, our God, we thank thee, and praise thy glorious name.
But who am I, and what is my people, that we should be able
to offer so willingly after this sort? For all things come of thee,
and of thine own have we given thee.*

(1 Chronicles 29:12–14)

*Every man also to whom God hath given riches and wealth,
and hath given him power to eat thereof, and to take his por-
tion, and to rejoice in his labour; this is the gift of God.*

(Ecclesiastes 5:19)

*Every good gift and every perfect gift is from above, and
cometh down from the Father of lights.*   (James 1:17)

God is the great giver and gives liberally to us all.

For God so love the world, that he gave his only begotten Son.

(John 3:16)

The gift of God is eternal life.   (Romans 6:23)

Thanks be unto God for his unspeakable gift.
                                    (2 Corinthians 9:15)

For by grace are ye saved through faith; and that not of your-selves: it is the gift of God.   (Ephesians 2:8)

God…giveth to all men liberally.   (James 1:5)

That ye may be the children of your Father which is in heaven: for he maketh his sun to rise on the evil and on the good, and sendeth rain on the just and on the unjust.   (Matthew 5:45)

All of God's great gifts come to us through His Son.

He that spared not his own Son, but delivered him up for us all, how shall he not with him also freely give us all things?
                                    (Romans 8:32)

Jesus Christ is a great giver, for He gave Himself for us.

For ye know the grace of our Lord Jesus Christ, that, though he was rich, yet for your sakes he became poor, that ye through his poverty might be rich.   (2 Corinthians 8:9)

Grace be to you and peace from God the Father, and from our Lord Jesus Christ, who gave himself for our sins, that he might deliver us from this present evil world, according to the will of God and our Father: to whom be glory for ever and ever. Amen.   (Galatians 1:3–5)

The Son of God, who loved me, and gave himself for me.
                                    (Galatians 2:20)

God has honored us by giving us the fruits of His creative hand. *"Blessed be the Lord, who daily loadeth us with benefits"* (Psalm 68:19). We are not worthy to receive these bounties, but God, the gracious Giver, has bestowed them on us!

So what shall you do?

God loveth a cheerful giver.   (2 Corinthians 9:7)

He that giveth, let him do it with simplicity. (Romans 12:8)

Now let's take a deeper look at what Scripture says about the giving heart.

1. *"Freely ye have received, freely give"* (Matthew 10:8). Have you discovered this fact? The more you give, the more you will want to give and the more you will have to give. Learn to be generous with what God has given you.

2. *"And all the tithe of the land, whether of the seed of the land, or of the fruit of the tree, is the* LORD's: *it is holy unto the* LORD" (Leviticus 27:30). Is 10 percent of what God has given you too much to ask for the work that you, as a Christian, claim to be the most important thing on earth? Try tithing for one year, and see the miracle of it all.

3. *"Cast thy bread upon the waters: for thou shalt find it after many days"* (Ecclesiastes 11:1). Forget about knowing the results and attend the sowing. Someday, you will be surprised at what giving can yield. God said, *"My word…shall not return unto me void"* (Isaiah 55:11).

4. *"Lay not up for yourselves treasures upon earth, where moth and rust doth corrupt, and where thieves break through and steal: but lay up for yourselves treasures in heaven, where neither moth nor rust doth corrupt, and where thieves do not break through nor steal"* (Matthew 6:19–20). One of the greatest drawbacks to Christianity is the Christian's savings account. Give what you can, while you can, to share the gospel of Christ, and forever you will be glad. The only thing we can take with us to heaven is what we have given away. If you are looking for lasting dividends, you had better deposit something in heaven.

5. *"And Jacob vowed a vow, saying, If God will be with me, and will keep me in this way that I go, and will give me bread to eat, and raiment to put on…then shall the* Lord *be my God: and this stone, which I have set for a pillar, shall be God's house: and of all that thou shalt give me I will surely give the tenth unto thee"* (Genesis 28:20, 22). There is something about getting right with God that involves giving. We owe God all our life and at least 10 percent of our income.

6. *"I have shewed you all things, how that so labouring ye ought to support the weak, and to remember the words of the Lord Jesus, how he said, It is more blessed to give than to receive"* (Acts 20:35). This has been called the most disbelieved verse in the Bible. Too bad! Disbelief withers the life of the disbeliever! Belief enriches the life of the believer! Get in on the giving end. That's where God is. Our gain is in giving, not holding back. Cheerfully give, and watch what God does. The feeling that comes with giving has no comparison. And, remember, you will never be able to top God in giving, no matter what or how much it is. Jesus said, *"Give, and it shall be given unto you"* (Luke 6:38).

7. *"But whoso hath this world's good, and seeth his brother have need, and shutteth up his bowels of compassion from him, how dwelleth the love of God in him?"* (1 John 3:17). Here is a question that can only be answered by action. Today, God will use you to help someone in need. See to it that you obey His voice. Jesus said, *"Inasmuch as ye have done it unto one of the least of these my brethren, ye have done it unto me"* (Matthew 25:40). Anyone wanting to do the Lord a special favor can do so with an act of kindness to the least of His children. *"Charity* [love] *suffereth long, and is kind"* (1 Corinthians 13:4). The poor have a special place in the heart of God. Be good to them.

16

YOUR WORTH: MORE THAN YOUR SALARY

E. W. KENYON

Put the company for which you work under obligation to you. Keep society under obligation to you. The world's greatest scientists, chemists, and mechanics have all put the world in debt to them.

Be a real contributor to your age. Don't just exist.

Fathers and mothers, give to the world some great sons and daughters. Put your best into their training. You have no idea how dependent the world is upon parents. Make the world a better place because you lived in it and played your part.

Selfishness cramps ability.

Be bigger than the blunders you make.

Live big.

Be big in your dreams, in all things you do.

Learn to love others.

Only those who love count.

Give to the world better service with every added year.

Forgive your enemies. Never go to their level and hate with them.

The lying and opposition of your enemies is your diploma.

Give a heaping measure in all your ministry.

God is the original Giver. Be in His class.

17

WHAT ARE YOU WORTH?

E. W. KENYON

What value do you place on yourself? Have you ever taken an inventory or said, "Well, I know I could do that," or "I believe I can sing better than that person," or "I believe I could build a business," or "I could be like that." Are you going to be what you could be? Honestly, are you worth anything in your own estimation? Have you set a price on yourself? Have you set a price on your own ability, on your own time? What is your word worth to yourself?

When you say, "I will get that lesson," "I will conquer that subject," "I will master that problem," is your word worth anything? Do you make your word come true when you say, "I will give that up; I will put that thing over"?

What is your word worth to you? Have you faith in your own word? I am not asking what your word is worth to others. Pride may make you keep your word with people, but do you keep your word with yourself?

You are too valuable to barter away the finest part of manhood or womanhood—your word. Likely, you are worth more to yourself than you are to anyone else; but in a year from now, can you make yourself so valuable that men will pay any price for you?

Great corporations are looking for men and women who can earn fifty thousand dollars a year. Set your mark—your standard—high, then go up there. Do not allow one day to go by in which you have not improved yourself. Take an inventory again and again, and see what you possess; see whether that possession is more valuable today than it was a year ago.

Find where your ability lies, then put all of your best into that ability and make it come across and put you over the top.

Remember that what you have hungered and yearned to do, you have the ability to do—if you will.

18

GOD GIVETH ME WEALTH AND HEALTH

DON GOSSETT

First, this "power poem" is one some will not easily trust. Some think it is unspiritual to have wealth, and some think that the gift of health is not likely to be obtained.

Second, the word *wealth* means resources, which come when you are competent to meet your obligations. God doesn't promise to make us millionaires, but He does provide for our every need (see Philippians 4:19), and assures us prosperity and good success if we live by His Word (see Joshua 1:8). If you delight in the Word of God and meditate on it, God says that whatever you do will prosper. (See Psalm 1:2–3.)

Third, Jesus said, "*Seek ye first the kingdom of God, and his right-eousness; and all these things shall be added unto you*" (Matthew 6:33). Jesus was speaking about our material provisions (food, raiment, and shelter). Jesus did not say that if we seek first the kingdom of God, all these things will be taken away from us. No, He said, "*All these things* [all our material provisions] *shall be added unto* [us]"!

Fourth, the Bible says, "*It is* [God] *that giveth thee the power to get wealth*" (Deuteronomy 8:18). And it is Satan's business to impoverish our lives, to ruin our Christian effectiveness in paying our obligations. Satan seeks to embarrass us in financial matters. Agree with God, disagree with the devil!

Fifth, God says, *"Beloved, I wish above all things that thou mayest prosper and be in health, even as thy soul prospereth"* (3 John 2). This is God's "big wish" for us, His children, that we may prosper and be in health, even as our souls prosper! How do we prosper in our souls? By engaging in Spirit-led prayer and having a positive praise life, by studying God's Word and confessing the Scriptures boldly, and by witnessing to others about Christ through our lives and lips.

Sixth, when so many of God's people are afflicted and poverty-stricken, and the work of God is reduced to a standstill, it's high time we affirm these Scriptures, to receive God's gifts of wealth and health.

Seventh, daily and boldly speak it: "God giveth me wealth and health"!

PART II:
FAITH FOR SUCCESS

19

BE LOOSED
FROM YOUR BONDAGE

DON GOSSETT

Three common bondages from which you ought to be loosed: sleeplessness, vexation, and fear. Remember: God is not the author of bondage, but of liberty. (See 2 Corinthians 3:17, Luke 4:18, Galatians 5:1.)

SLEEPLESSNESS

"For so he giveth his beloved sleep" (Psalm 127:2). God is the Giver of sleep. He knows our need of good, sound sleep at night. Satan is the author of insomnia. Jesus revealed him to be a thief (see John 10:10) who steals; he seeks to rob us of sleep. Sleeplessness breeds nervous disorders, depression, physical infirmities. Positively, God giveth His beloved sleep! Take your sleep from our good God who richly gives us all things to enjoy. (See 1 Timothy 6:17; James. 1:17.) Refuse the devil's gift of insomnia. Quote this Word: "I will both lay me down in peace and sleep: for thou, LORD, only makest me dwell in safety" (Psalm 4:8).

VEXATION

The Bible often mentions being vexed by unclean spirits. This word *vex* means to obsess, harass, or mob. Satan vexes your mind with impure thoughts, worry and frustration. He vexes you spiritually by hindering your freedom in prayer, worship and witnessing. He vexes you with wrong spirits that produce complaining, lying, pride; also a love of self, the praise of men, the world, money or eating intemperately. You needn't ask God to cast out these vexing spirits from your life. You can do it. *"Resist the devil and he will flee from you"* (James 4:7). "In My name shall ye cast out devils," declared Jesus. (See Mark 16:17.) *"The truth shall make you free"* (John 8:32).

FEAR

Are you experiencing a fear of death, fear of failure, fear of old age, fear of sickness, fear of poverty, or fear of calamity? Likely, you face often *"the fear of man which bringeth a snare"* (Proverbs 29:25). These spirits of fear do not originate from God. (See 2 Timothy 1:7.) They are Satan's "gifts" to you. Don't accept them any longer! Refuse them in Jesus' name. Receive God's gifts of power, love and a sound mind.

Affirm right now, *"I will walk at liberty"* (Psalm 119:45). Jesus indignantly declared that every child of God ought to *"be loosed"* (Luke 13:16) from every bondage of Satan. Boldly walk in liberty! Praise the Lord for loosening your life!

20

PUTTING YOURSELF IN THE WAY OF SUCCESS

E. W. KENYON

If only I could repeat it over and over again, so that, wherever you turned in this book, your eyes would see this one fact: You have within you all of the qualities and elements that are necessary to make you a success. Your chief work is the development of the thing that nature has already given you.

Before you go to your place of business, create all around you and in you an atmosphere of victory.

You go out with the consciousness that you have victory. You and the unseen One are going to your place of business together, and you are going to put it over.

You are going out after that job with the smile of a victor—not the smile of one who is trying to smile, but one who smiles in spite of him or herself.

Cultivate the habit of thorough work. If it is mental work, think every problem through. Be the one person in the place where you work who thinks through on every problem that arises.

You will find that your boss will want you.

Few others have the ability to think through.

They guess; they speculate; they theorize.

But you are the kind of person who takes a problem and resolutely drives yourself to think through that problem from every angle.

The boss can get others to do what he tells them to do. He is looking for one with ability to tell others how to do it.

So set the standard high for yourself.

Have a lofty spiritual idea. Climb to it.

Between you and it, there may be many a swamp through which a road must be made.

Lumbermen always build roads to the timber they wish to market.

You will have to build a road to market your abilities.

There is pain and fatigue ahead for you, but you dress for the job.

Remember to associate with people who have won, those who help you climb to the top.

Don't hang around with a group of "has beens." Associate with the men and women who are climbing up.

The idle, gossiping people will not help you.

The lazy and careless will stand in your way.

Those who spend their nights in the roadhouse or at the gambling hall will never help you.

Don't think you can get something for nothing.

Put your money where it will count.

Put your time where it will pay you dividends.

The battle is not for the thoughtless, heedless guesser or the idealistic dreamer.

It is for the man or woman who works.

21

HOW TO RECEIVE GUIDANCE FROM GOD

DON GOSSETT

Trust in the LORD *with all thine heart; and lean not unto thine own understanding. In all thy ways acknowledge him, and he shall direct thy paths.* (Proverbs 3:5–6)

Thy word is a lamp unto my feet, and a light unto my path. (Psalm 119:105)

All guidance must be in harmony with the Word of God, never apart from it. The Holy Spirit always uses the Word—*"Taking the sword of the Spirit, which is the word of God"* (Ephesians 6:17).

For instance, the Holy Spirit never leads a Christian to marry a non-Christian, for that would be a violation of God's Word: *"Be ye not unequally yoked with unbelievers"* (2 Corinthians 6:14). The Holy Spirit never leads a true Christian to walk in darkness— never. Jesus said, *"I am the light of the world: he that followeth me shall not walk in darkness"* (John 8:12).

We should not make guidance complicated. *"A man's heart deviseth his way: but the Lord directeth his steps"* (Proverbs 16:9).

We must submit to His lordship over our lives. *"Trust in the Lord with all thine heart."* Confess it by saying, "Jesus is Lord; I trust Him with all my heart."

We must resist the enemy by using the authority of Jesus to silence the voice of the enemy. *"Resist the devil, and he will flee from you"* (James 4:7).

Because we are His sheep, we can expect to have His guidance. *"My sheep hear my voice, and I know them, and they follow me"* (John 10:27).

Allow God to speak the way He chooses. Pray as did Samuel: *"Speak, Lord; for thy servant heareth"* (1 Samuel 3:9). God may choose to speak by an audible voice (see Exodus 3:4–5) or by dreams (see Matthew 2:13, 22) or by visions (see Isaiah 6:1; Revelation 1:12–17).

One of the most unusual ways God gives guidance is revealed in Isaiah 30:21: *"And thine ears shall hear a word behind thee, saying, This is the way, walk ye in it, when ye turn to the right hand, and when ye turn to the left."*

Get your own leading from God. Beware of counterfeit guidance. The Lord may use others to confirm your guidance.

22

FULL ASSURANCE OF FAITH

DON GOSSETT

After I received Jesus Christ by faith into my life, there were yet times that I had doubts about my salvation. These doubts were caused by unsaved people who jeered the Bible and things of God. Also, I often pondered if I had the right "feelings" a Christian should have. Then, too, when I would fail the Lord, I wondered if there was anything to my supposedly being saved.

But in my quest, God gave me the *"full assurance of faith"* (Hebrews 10:22) and cured me of all my doubt. Praise His name. How did I attain this full assurance of faith? From God's wonderful Word!

"Nobody can know for sure he is saved." This is what I was told by a man I once met and with whom I shared my knowledge of salvation through Christ.

"Never in this life can a person know he is saved," the man continued. "You just must keep on doing the best you can, and when the books are opened, you will find out whether you made it or not."

This worried me. I was trying my best to be a Christian. What if this man is right? As a youngster, this really bothered me.

I cannot say the full understanding of my sure relationship with God came instantly. Rather, it was a matter of learning *"the truth, and the truth shall make you free"* (John 8:32), declared Jesus.

Peace with God. I'm glad I'm a Christian because of the peace with God I gained when I accepted Christ by faith. *"Therefore being justified by faith, we have peace with God through our Lord Jesus Christ"* (Romans 5:1). As long as I resisted the call of the Spirit to accept Christ as my Savior, I was warring against God; I was His enemy, even though He loved me. But then when I ceased resisting and by faith received Him, I had peace with God!

Full Authority to Know. *"As many as received him, to them gave he power to become the sons of God, even to them that believe on his name"* (John 1:12). I received Christ; therefore I knew I was a son of God, His own child. This power I received had changed me, transformed me, made me anew. Hallelujah! O the wonder of receiving Christ, then knowing I was saved.

Another great truth that gave me victory over doubts was this one: *"The Spirit itself beareth witness with our spirit, that we are the children of God"* (Romans 8:16). I received the witness of the Spirit of God that I belonged to Him. This was precious to know.

Doubts are only cast out by truth. And the truth of God did its work in my heart. *"We know that we have passed from death unto life, because we love the brethren"* (1 John 3:14). When I was saved and knew it, I discovered that hate, grudges, and unforgiveness toward those who had wronged me were gone. I loved others, especially fellow Christians, but God also enabled me to love those who, in the natural order of things, I didn't like. Thank God for His love that passes understanding.

It is not presumption to declare, here and now in this life, that one is saved. *"He that hath the Son hath life"* (1 John 5:12). I knew I had received the Son of God into my heart, and I knew His divine life was within me.

> *Therefore if any man be in Christ, he is a new creature: old things are passed away; behold, all things are become new.*
> (2 Corinthians 5:17)

God declares this is His Word. I knew I was a new creature in Christ. This was by His grace, through faith in Jesus Christ.

God had said so, and *"God is not a man, that he should lie"* (Numbers 23:19).

I have deep assurance that one day I will meet Christ face-to-face. My assurance doesn't rest on feelings alone, but on God's Word. And His Word is like an anchor; it holds me steadfast and sure!

23

GLADNESS:
A SECRET TO STRENGTH

DON GOSSETT

Greater than any human pleasure or happiness is the joy of the Lord. Joyful Christians are the best advertisement for Christianity. Joyful Christians have always been a challenge and testimonial to a broken-hearted world.

Happiness is the product of our surroundings. It is the thing that satisfies the senses. The material things that bring a man happiness may be taken away in a moment, and he is left desolate.

Joy belongs to the spiritual realm, just as happiness belongs to the sense realm. When a Christian is not joyful, it is either because of broken fellowship or a lack of knowledge of what he is in Christ. It is this unspeakable joy that makes you triumphant over the petty trials of life, and a victor over the testings that may come.

John said the purpose of our fellowship life was that we might have fullness of joy. (See 1 John 1:3–4.) Joy cannot be full without full fellowship. It is this joy that makes Christianity the most attractive thing in the world. When joy goes away, the Word loses its power, its freshness and richness. It is only when fellowship is at floodtide and your heart filled with joy that God is honored and souls are saved.

Fellowship in its fullness is the joyful life with the throttle wide open on a down grade. Yes, this joy of the Lord is one of the greatest things that comes to us in the new birth. It makes trouble lose its grip upon us; it makes poverty lose its terror.

Remember, Jesus said, *"My joy I give to you"* (John 15:11).

Again we consider the difference between joy and happiness. Both are to be desired, but it is far more important that we have joy than merely earthly happiness. Happiness depends on the things that we have or own, like property or loved ones. But joy is a thing of the spirit. It is an artesian well in the spirit that bubbles up and overflows. It is the thing that comes as a result of the Spirit's working in our lives.

We read that the martyrs had joy unspeakable, even when dying in physical agony. It was a joy that stirred the multitudes and startled men: How could they be so full of joy when they knew that death was near?

I've witnessed many Christians going through deep sorrow, but have been kept by this unquenchable joy.

In years of evangelism, I've observed that joy is the real secret. In our meetings, I've noticed that it is the joyful, living testimony that stirs the people. It is the person who is so full of joy that he can hardly speak, as the tears stream down his face that moves the people. Yes, it is indeed the joyful testimony that touches hearts.

When we speak the Word with assurance and joy, it brings conviction to the listeners. When the Word becomes more real to you than any word many have ever spoken, your lips will be filled with laughter, your heart will be filled with joy, and you will have a victorious Christian life.

How many times I have seen that the hesitant testimony is a forerunning of failure, and the joyful testimony is forerunner of victory.

Christians are only as strong as they are filled with joy of the Lord. A church is only as strong and influential for Christ as its community is filled with the real joy of the Lord. Why? *"The joy of the Lord is your strength"* (Nehemiah 8:10). When people complain of lacking strength, or talk about how weak they are, often their real lack is the joy of the Lord.

When the Israelites returned from Babylon to rebuild the walls of Jerusalem, Nehemiah found many of them were mourning and weeping; some were suffering with diseases; others were weak and undernourished. Not a few were downcast, defeated and despondent. But Nehemiah asked God for help for his people, and God gave them the message through their leader: *"This day is holy unto the Lord your God; mourn not, nor weep. For all the people wept…. Neither be ye sorry; for the joy of the Lord is your strength"* (Nehemiah 8:9–10).

"The joy of the Lord is your strength"! This was God's answer for Israel then; it is God's answer for us today.

The joy of the Lord is not just a byproduct the Lord gives us. It is in actuality *"the joy of the Lord."* It is not a selfish attribute to want to be full of the joy of the Lord. Christ Himself *"who for the joy that was set before him endured the cross, despising the shame, and is set down at the right hand of the throne of God"* (Hebrews 12:2).

This joy of the Lord is our strength, and is a vital characteristic in receiving and maintaining good health and success. This joy is not only strength spiritually, but likewise, it ministers physical and mental strength to us.

24

SOME THINGS THAT ARE BEGOTTEN OF GOD

E. W. KENYON

The new creation is begotten of God. Righteousness is begotten of God. Love is begotten of God. Faith is begotten of God. These are the overcomers of the world.

> *Who is he that overcometh the world, but he that believeth that Jesus is the Son of God?* (1 John 5:5 ASV)

If you believe this, you are a victor. The believers are winners.

Leave the lowlands of doubt and fear, and come out onto the highlands to walk in fellowship with God. Healing and victory are yours. Leave failure to the failures.

> *Nay, in all* [our fights] *we are more than conquerors.*
> (Romans 8:37 ASV)

Why? Because we are raised together with Christ. When Jesus arose from the dead, it was our victory over the enemy. Conybeare's translation of Colossians 2:15 tells us this: "And He disarmed the Principalities and Powers [which fought against

Him], and put them to open shame, leading them captive in the triumph of Christ."[2]

You remember that we were crucified with Him, we died with Him, we were buried with Him, we suffered with Him, we were justified with Him, and we were made alive with Him. Then we met the enemy, and we conquered him in Christ.

So Paul can say to us: *"Wherein ye were also raised with him through faith in the working of God, who raised him from the dead"* (Colossians 2:12 asv).

God raised Christ so that we might share in His life.

We were made partakers in Christ's resurrection life, Christ's resurrection victory, and Christ's resurrection new creation.

Of his fulness we all received.   (John 1:16 asv)

For we are his workmanship, created in Christ Jesus.
                                        (Ephesians 2:10 asv)

---

2. William John Conybeare and John Saul Howson, *The Life and Epistles of St. Paul: (Vol. 1)*, 479.

25

WAILING AND FAILING GO HAND IN HAND

DON GOSSETT

The Lord promised me a saved life, a healed life, and a Spirit-filled life. Here He promises me a life of blessings if I "keep" my mouth and tongue. If I wail about my health, my finances, and my family, I will surely fail.

> *Whoso offereth praise glorifieth me: and to him that ordereth his conversation aright will I shew the salvation of God.*
> (Psalm 50:23)

To "ordereth [my] *conversation aright*" is to refuse wailing as the standard of my conversation. Wailing is negative, complaining, fault-finding speech. If I do not wail, I will not fail. Then God will bless me with the full benefits of His salvation—healing, deliverance, protection, and provision.

> *Thou art snared with the words of thy mouth, thou art taken [captive] with the words of thy mouth.* (Proverbs 6:2)

Wailing will entrap my soul and invariably lead me into captivity.

Death and life are in the power of the tongue.

(Proverbs 18:21)

Wailing is speaking "*death*" to my circumstances, my home, my ministry, and my relationships.

If any man among you seem to be religious, and bridleth not his tongue, but deceiveth his own heart, that man's religion is vain. (James 1:26)

If I wail, it's because I have an unbridled tongue, which leads to self-deception and a worthless walk with the Lord.

Can two walk together, except they be agreed? (Amos 3:3)

Wailing is an indication of not walking in agreement with God's Word. Agreeing is saying what God says about my life, fulfilling the Lord's will.

Wailing and failing go hand in hand!

I am purposed that my mouth shall not transgress.

(Psalm 17:3)

I said, I will take heed to my ways, that I sin not with my tongue: I will keep my mouth with a bridle. (Psalm 39:1)

What man is he that desireth life, and loveth many days, that he may see good? Keep thy tongue from evil, and thy lips from speaking guile. (Psalm 34:12–13)

I love life! I desire to see many good days. I will train my tongue to not wail and fail! "I overcome Satan by the blood of the Lamb and the word of my testimony." (See Revelation 12:11.)

Joe was jealous. His suspicious mistrust of another caused him to engage in unpleasant wailing. Marie had deep resentment that caused her to lament her displeasure and indignation for having been offended. Kevin vocally expressed his bitterness with biting sarcasm and sharpness of speech. Nellie expressed her animosity toward others with words of active hostility. John mourned his self-pity caused by a sense of frustration over life's insolvable problems. All five of these "wailing wall Christians" were failures in life. Lamenting, mournful speech, words spoken in despair, are forerunners of failure.

> *For by thy words thou shalt be justified, and by thy words thou shalt be condemned.* (Matthew 12:37)

26

YOU HAVE IT IN YOU

E. W. KENYON

No one can put you in to the realm of success but you. No one can compel you to cooperate with the laws of victory but you.

You have God in you. You have His wisdom and grace and ability. You have a right to draw upon the resources of God. They are all yours. His wisdom is yours. His strength is yours. His love is yours. His grace is yours. What more do you need?

No one can do it for you. You alone can develop abilities in yourself. You alone can turn dreams into realities. No one can press the button but you.

Self-discipline is self-education. It is driving yourself to study the Word, to a life of prayer, to soul-winning. No one can do it for you.

Be your own alarm clock. Buy your own gas and stop depending on others for inspiration. Get out of the habit of hitchhiking.

Come over into the realm of victory, where you belong. Be a stern boss over yourself. This is imperative.

Drive yourself to think through your situations. The lazy-minded man is always hard up. He trusts others to think for him.

Remember that it is the *you* in you that puts you over the top. You make your mind do its work. You learn how to use knowledge and make it worthwhile.

You know that "Jesus was made wisdom unto you." (See 1 Corinthians 1:30.) Now you must take advantage of it. Perhaps you have gathered a considerable amount of knowledge, but it is of no value without wisdom. Jesus is made unto you wisdom.

Make your best a better best. This is the real game, and the ultimate prize is greater joy.

The ability to help folks is in you. Now develop yourself and go to it.

27

SPEAK SUCCESS, NOT FAILURE

DON GOSSETT

Speak a new creation, not the old creation filled with envy and rottenness. Declare it: "I am a new creature in Christ Jesus; the old things are passed away; behold all things are become new." (See 2 Corinthians 5:17.)

Speak your righteousness in Christ, not unworthiness. Affirm it: "I am the righteousness of God in Christ Jesus." (See 2 Corinthians 5:21.)

Speak the language of the new kingdom of God's dear Son in which you now dwell, not the old kingdom of darkness from which you have been translated. *"Giving thanks unto the Father, which hath made us meet to be partakers of the inheritance of the saints in light: who hath delivered us from the power of darkness, and hath translated us into the kingdom of his dear Son: in whom we have redemption through his blood, even the forgiveness of sins"* (Colossians 1:12–14).

Speak that you are an heir of God and a joint heir with Jesus Christ, not your old identification as a captive to sin and Satan. Testify to it: "I have a rich inheritance. I am blessed with every spiritual blessing. The Father Himself loveth me." (See Ephesians 1:3.)

Speak that you have the life of God in your mortal body, not the old spirit of inferiority, failure, and frustration. "In Christ you live and move and have your being." (See Acts 17:28.)

Speak healing and health, not how sick and diseased you are. Isaiah 33:24 foretells a future time when *"the inhabitant shall not say, I am sick."* That's a good practice in kingdom living now. Don't say, "I am sick," but speak the Word that heals. "With His stripes I am healed." (See Isaiah 53:5.)

Speak financial success, not poverty and misery. Speak marriage success, not marriage failure. *"Then thou shalt make thy way prosperous, and then thou shalt have good success"* (Joshua 1:8).

28

WE HAVE COME TO KNOW THAT THE LOVE WAY IS BEST

E. W. KENYON

*And we have known and believed the love that God hath to us.
God is love; and he that dwelleth in love dwelleth in God, and
God in him.* (1 John 4:16)

We have come to know the Love Way is best. We have come to believe in love. We believe it is better than force, better than argument, better than money, and better than going to court. It has been hard for us to believe in God's love for us when difficulties came into our lives, but we know now that all of these abnormal things are not the product of love. They come from the Adversary seeking to dethrone love in our hearts. The Bible has much to say about the real you. Not the tent you see in the mirror, but the eternal you, who is more than a conqueror in Christ: Through Love.

For us to become God-inside minded is for us to become victors. As soon as we become God-inside conscious, we will begin to depend upon the God inside. We will know that *"greater is he that is in you, than he that is in the world"* (1 John 4:4).

There will be a holy boldness in us, a Jesus-like fearlessness. No matter what happens to us, He is inside and He will take us over. We have His ability, His courage, and His strength. It takes us out of the failure realm, and puts us over into the realm of success.

> *For if, through the transgression of the one individual, Death made use of the one individual to seize the sovereignty, all the more shall those who receive God's overflowing grace and the gift of righteousness reign as kings in Life through the one individual, Jesus Christ.* (Romans 5:17 WEY)

We have received the gift of righteousness. We have received the abundance of grace. We reign as kings in the realm of life or love.

Love takes us away from the sense of inferiority and gives us the sense of our oneness with Christ. The old inferiority complex that comes from sin-consciousness has been destroyed. Love-consciousness and Son-consciousness have taken its place.

One cannot have a servile spirit and enjoy the reality of Sonship. We are masters; we are conquerors; we are overcomers because we are one with Him. We have His ability, His wisdom, His strength, His love. Spiritually, we are free men. We abide in God, and God abides in us. Waiting before the Lord for power, or for some special blessing that you have heard about is unnecessary because you have in you, if you have received the Holy Spirit, the Fountain of all experiences.

We have His ability, His wisdom, His strength, His love.

29

OVERCOME YOUR INFERIORITY COMPLEX

DON GOSSETT

Why should you be inferior? You know the secret of the Christian life is not in yourself, but in the Christ who indwells you. The Bible makes it clear: you are in Christ and Christ is in you. The very word Christian means we are "Christin people." We are not Christian workers, we are Christ containers. Say it, *"Nevertheless I live; yet not I, but Christ liveth in me: and the life which I now live in the flesh I live by the faith of the Son of God, who loved me, and gave himself for me"* (Galatians 2:20).

When you are aware that Christ lives in you, there is nothing inferior about Him and He is your life. Colossians 3:4, *"When Christ, who is our life, shall appear, then shall ye also appear with him in glory."* Paul tells us sixty-seven times that we are in Christ.

You can overcome your inferiority complex if you simply yield to Christ. The Christian life is not a struggle, it is a yielding process. *"Yield yourselves unto God"* (Romans 6:13). Let Christ live His life in you. You will overcome your inferiority complex by the joyful awareness that Jesus Christ indwells you by His Spirit.

"*Let the redeemed of the* LORD *say so*" (Psalm 107:2). Christianity is a "*say so*" thing. "*With the mouth confession is made unto salvation*" (Romans 10:10). Your confession precedes your possession. You cannot rise higher than your confession. A wrong confession will imprison you, but a right confession will set you free.

"*Let the weak say, I am strong*" (Joel 3:10). Confess it, "I am strong!"

Let the defeated say, "*God...always causeth us to triumph in Christ*" (2 Corinthians 2:14).

Let the apologetic say, "*I know whom I have believed, and am persuaded that he is able to keep that which I have committed unto him against that day*" (2 Timothy 1:12).

Let the timid say, "*If God be for us, who can be against us?*" (Romans 8:31).

Let the fearful say, "*The Lord is my helper, and I will not fear what man shall do unto me*" (Hebrews 13:6).

You do not have to struggle through life bound with an inferiority complex. How can you be inferior when you know your rights in Christ? How can you be "complexed" as a Christian when you count on this fact: "*Not that we are sufficient of ourselves to think any thing as of ourselves; but our sufficiency is of God*" (2 Corinthians 3:5).

What you say is what you get. You get victory over an inferiority complex when you say these things: "I overcome an inferiority complex through Christ, His Word, and His sufficiency. By divine birth I am linked up with Jesus Christ; there is nothing inferior about Him! I am who God says I am. I have what God says I have. I can do what God says I can do."

30

UNDERESTIMATING JESUS

E. W. KENYON

One cannot conceive of anything that will cripple faith and put the believer in bondage more quickly and surely than underestimating what He is, and what we are in Him. Along with that will come an underestimation of the Word.

We will say, "Oh, I believe the Bible is the Word of God," and yet we turn to the arm of flesh for help. And when we pray, we do not come with that quiet assurance that we would if some banker had given us his word in regard to our financial standing at the bank. This is an unconscious underestimation of the Word, and it is an unconscious underestimation of the integrity of the Master Himself, who is the Author of this Word. This leads to weakness, to doubt and fear. It makes a vacillating type of faith.

We become what James calls *"a double minded man [that] is unstable in all his ways"* (James 1:8). What will change it? When we realize what He has done for us in His great substitution and in the new creation. We should meditate on the fact that we are partakers of the divine nature. *"These things have I written unto you that believe on the name of the Son of God; that ye may know that ye have eternal life, and that ye may believe on the name of the Son of God"* (1 John 5:13).

If we say over and over again to our hearts, "I am a partaker of God's very nature. I have in me His faith nature. This makes me a child of faith. I have been begotten of the Living Word through the Holy Spirit. The real me was recreated in Christ. I have the very nature of the Father and the Father is love, so I have in me the love nature of the Father," if we meditate on this, we will no longer be *"double minded"* men.

Repeat it over and over again. Hold it as a constant affirmation before your mind that you are what He says you are; that you are a partaker of His very nature as He has declared. And you remember that *"greater is he that is in you, than he that is in the world"* (1 John 4:4). That Greater One is the Holy Spirit.

The Holy Spirit is the One that in creation gave the color, the beauty and fragrance to the flowers, to vegetation, to the trees. He is the One that takes of the nature of the Father, and through the Word, builds it into us. He builds the beauty of Christ into our conduct.

He touches our reasoning faculties until the things that He has made in the floral world assume a new interest and their beauty is enhanced and their fragrance enjoyed as never before. I can remember the night that I received eternal life. It seemed as though I hardly touched the sidewalk on my way home. It was a cold winter night in January, but, oh, how beautiful the snow and the frost. Yes, the trees stripped of their foliage assumed a beauty I had never noted before. The Holy Spirit had taken possession and was unveiling the wonders of His grace to me.

An underestimation of the Holy Spirit, of the Word, of Jesus, will keep us in a state of flux, in a realm of uncertainty. Fear will dominate us; doubt will bind us, and hold us in the realm of weakness. But when we come to know Jesus as our Lord, as the Mighty One at the right hand of the Father who ever lives to make intercession for us, our great Lawyer that looks after every legal need of ours in Christ, we will no longer be dominated by fear and doubt. We should come to know the reality of the Holy Spirit's reality, which is all unveiled to us in the Pauline revelation.

I urge you to go back and read Romans and first and second Corinthians again. Then abide a while in Ephesians, in those first three chapters especially, until you are lifted out of the realm of the senses into the realm of the new man in Christ Jesus.

The fear of seeing what we are in Christ, and of acting as though we knew what we were, has kept us in bondage and robbed us of the reality of His finished work. How slow we have been to act what we are in Him. The Spirit, through the Word, has declared what we are in Christ. *"In whom we have our redemption through his blood, the forgiveness of sins"* (Ephesians 1:7), and it is according to the riches of His grace.

This is not a theological redemption. This is not Paul's philosophy. This is the Father's description of what we are in His Son, and He says *"in whom we have our redemption."* From whom and what are we redeemed?

WHAT HE MADE US

Satan is the god of darkness. We have been delivered out of Satan's dominion, out of the realm and authority of darkness. We have been delivered out of the dominion of sin, for *"sin shall not have dominion over you"* (Romans 6:14). We are delivered out of the authority of disease, for Romans 8:11 says, *"If the Spirit of him that raised up Jesus from the dead dwell in you, he that raised up Christ from the dead shall also quicken your mortal bodies by his Spirit that dwelleth in you."*

Not only have we a redemption that is literal and absolute, but we are a new creation, and Satan has no dominion over us. Jesus is the Head and Lord of this new creation.

We have been taught so long and so persistently about our weaknesses and our lack of ability and our unworthiness that we hardly dare say that we are what He says we are. We are afraid that people will misunderstand us and think that we have become fanatical.

But He says: "*Therefore if any man is in Christ* [and we are in Christ], *he is a new creature: old things are passed away; behold, all things are become new. And all things are of God*" (2 Corinthians 5:17–18) and we are reconciled to Him. We are a part of His very dream. Satan has no dominion over this new creation.

Ephesians 2:10 says we are created in Christ Jesus, that when Jesus arose from the dead the work of the new creation was consummated in Christ. It became a reality in us when we took Him as our Savior and confessed Him as our Lord.

The Father, in His Word, has declared what we are in His Son. That declaration is the truth. I may not have grown up to it, may not have appreciated it, but it stands there with an open door inviting me to enjoy all the fullness that is mine in Him. He declares what we may do in the name of His Son. We haven't appreciated it perhaps, but He gave to us the power of attorney to use His Son's name. Jesus said, "*Hitherto have ye asked nothing in my name: ask, and ye shall receive, that your joy may be full*" (John 16:24).

Seven times Jesus repeats this, giving us the legal right to the use of His name.

Philippians 2:9–10 tells us that this name is above every name, and at the name of Jesus every knee should bow, beings in heaven, beings on earth, and beings under the earth, and every tongue shall confess that Jesus is Lord to the glory of God my Father.

Not only that, but Jesus said after He arose from the dead, "*All authority hath been given unto me in heaven and on earth. Go ye therefore, and make disciples of all the nations*" (Matthew 18:18–19 ASV). Disciple means a student, a learner. He never said, "Go and make converts;" he never said, "Go and make churches;" but he said, "Go...*and make disciples.*"

There will be schools of Christ. Every believer will be a student of this living Word. What masters they will be! Not only do we have that power to use the name of Jesus to cast out demons, or to heal the sick, but that name gives us access to the Father, and is the absolute guarantee of answered prayer. You see, this prayer life is based upon absolute knowledge. It is not based upon emotion or feelings or the theories of men, but upon the living Word of God, this Word that *"liveth and abideth for ever"* (1 Peter 1:23).

When you know in your heart that you are what He says you are, then you act it in the face of all, confessing what He has done in you, confessing what He has made you. This glorifies Him and His work. To deny what we are, to tell what Satan is doing in our bodies and minds, is denying what we are in Christ.

When Jesus said, *"All things are possible to him that believeth"* (Mark 9:23), He meant that all things are possible to the believer. All that believer needs to do is to get to know what he is in Christ, then rise up and take his place.

What masters He has made us to be! How invincible we are! Can't you see what it would mean for one in the face of all this to be talking about weakness or lack, making a confession of inability? *"Of his fulness have all we received"* (John 1:16), and it is grace and the ability of God for us to enjoy to the very limit all that we are in Him.

31

FACING LIFE AS IT IS

E. W. KENYON

Don't say, "If things were different, I would do something." Do something with them as they are. Facing your life as it is now and winning is the object.

When things get hard and money stops coming in, or you lose your job and everything goes wrong, take account of stock. See what is wrong. See what you have forgotten and then go on and conquer.

You dream what you would do if.... Now wipe out the "if." Dream, and do it regardless of circumstances.

You say, "That cannot be done." It can be done. There is no "can't" about it. The man who wills to do it, who is willing to do the work and puts up the fight, can put it over.

A young man discovered a vein of gold high up on a mountain. He needed power. He needed money. He needed to know how to develop it. He struggled and worked and failed.

Sitting down one night after a long, hard day, tired through and through, he said to himself, "I know where my difficulty is—I don't know anything about this rock. I don't know anything about geology, and I know nothing about mining. I am going down to the city to find out."

He went down to the city to the head of the mining department at the university and laid the case before him. The professor called up a mining engineer. The young man met with the engineer and told him his story. After, the engineer said that he must go and see the vein.

It took about a week to get there. After the engineer had seen it, he said, "There are millions there, but it will cost a great deal to get in here and develop it. You will have to organize a stock company or sell it. Which will you do?"

The young man said, "I am going to develop it."

It took him a year of hard training and study, but he gave himself utterly to it. Through the long winter months, he drove himself until, when springtime came, he had acquired the knowledge that he needed. And it made him millions.

The trouble with too many people is that they want to get it too easily. Most of us say, "If I'd had a chance, I would have done it, but circumstances were against me. I don't have an education. I didn't have the pull." We associate our failure with the lack of opportunity.

The fellow in this story, handicapped worse than we, made opportunities. He fought until opportunities came to him. Success belongs to the man who simply wills to do it. He is the man who makes success come his way.

The fellow who lies down and says, "I can't do it," is a failure.

Don't lose heart if the first efforts fail. Go back and find the reason. Pick up the wreckage of old failures and build them into successes. You can do it.

32

HOW TO PRAY AND GET RESULTS

DON GOSSETT

First, prayer is the way that God has chosen to work on behalf of humanity. However, God will do little or nothing for us unless we ask Him. (See James 4:2.) He says, *"Call unto me, and I will answer thee"* (Jeremiah 33:3). Real prayer is simply asking God and expecting to receive an answer!

Second, *"come boldly unto the throne of grace, that we may obtain mercy, and find grace to help in time of need"* (Hebrews 4:16). The biblical way to come to God is with boldness. This means that we have confidence and assurance that we are very welcome. Then we remove hindrances to receiving answers in our lives, such as an unclean heart and a wrong spirit. Confess your sins to God (see 1 John 1:9) and ask Him to renew within you a right spirit (see Psalm 51:10).

Third, who can pray and get results? Paul did. So did Daniel, David, Elijah, and Abraham. Why? Because *"the effectual fervent prayer of a righteous man availeth much"* (James 5:16). So who is righteous today? You are! Knowing that you are righteous is the greatest foundation of a prayer life that gets results. Your being righteous is based only on what Jesus has done for you. (See 2 Corinthians 5:21; Romans 10:10.) As a righteous person, you have influence with God! The prayer of the righteous gets results! What does it means to be righteous? It means you have the ability to stand in God's presence without any sense of sin, guilt, or unworthiness. You come boldly into God's presence through the blood of Jesus. (See Hebrews 10:19.)

Fourth, pray about everything. (See Philippians 4:6.) Dare to ask God for miracles. (See John 16:23–24.) *"When ye pray, believe that ye receive them, and ye shall have them"* (Mark 11:24). Only believing prayer gets results from God. Ask the Father in Jesus' name. Then believe you have received...and you shall have! Then shift from praying to praising when you are fully persuaded that, what God has promised, He will perform! (See Romans 4:21.)

Fifth, cease struggling. You have committed your need into God's hands, so rest in the sure promises of God. You have *"planted"* your request in prayer; so *"water"* it with much praise and expect God to give the *"increase"*! (See 1 Corinthians 3:6–8.) And He will!

33

KEEP AT IT

E. W. KENYON

How did you ever do it? I can't see how anyone could do a thing like that."

I was in a curio shop with a friend of mine, and on the table was a whole army of little figures that had been whittled by hand. What hours of work must have been spent on them.

My friend stood there and, looking at them, asked the artist, "How did you ever do it?"

He smiled and said, "I just kept at it."

As I walked the street, I heard those three words replay in my mind. "Kept at it." "Kept at it." "Kept at it." How they ran through my soul. That man had kept at it. He had put life into it. He had made a success.

People were coming from all parts of the country to see the effect of that cultivated, trained genius. And all that man had done was train his mind and hand, and then whittle his dreams out of wood, soft stone, and ivory.

I was thrilled through and through at the possibilities wrapped up in common folk like you and me.

I once heard a girl play the piano. She was not over sixteen. I know something about music. We had a music department in our institution for many years. I looked into her face and whispered in my own heart, *Girl, you have spent hours pounding the keys while other girls were walking the street. While others were sleeping and Mother was trying to get them out of bed, you were pounding those keys. You have lost a heap of good times, but what a musician you are!*

She kept at it. That's why she won.

I stood with a man overlooking a beautiful farm in northern Maine. I asked him, "Who cleared this land? Who stumped it?"

He answered, "Do you see that little log house down there by the creek? I built that, and my wife and I moved into it before there was an acre of this land cleared. I vowed that I would clear every acre of it and put it into crops, and I have done it."

That is the spirit that conquers—"I vowed I would do it, and I have done it."

I stood by the loom in a factory as a boy and vowed that I would become an educator. I did not know what kind of educator, but I knew that within me was a teaching gift, an undeveloped thing. I vowed that I would do it, and I did. I was handicapped as few men have been handicapped, but I did it.

I am passing it on to you to show that the world cannot conquer you if you will to do it. Struggle to improve. In every effort, improve your dream. Every time you play that piece on the piano, play it better than you played it before. Every time you sit down at a typewriter, make up your mind to be more efficient than you have ever been.

Make your brain work. It will sweat, but make it work. It will improve. It will develop until you become a wonder to those around you.

Don't depend on an alarm clock. Don't depend on your mother waking you. Make up your mind that you will have an alarm clock in your soul.

Never depend on another man's car. Get one of your own. Be self-reliant. Be punctual. Be diligent. Think through every problem. Conquer your difficulties as a part of the day's job.

We are out in the fight, and we will win the crown!

34

THREE OF THE GREATEST, GRANDEST, AND MOST WONDERFUL THINGS I KNOW

DON GOSSETT

1. We are who God says we are!

A new creature: *"If any man be in Christ, he is a **new creature**"* (2 Corinthians 5:17).

*"[God] hath **delivered** us from the power of darkness"* (Colossians 1:13).

Overcomers: *"And they **overcame** [Satan] by the blood of the Lamb, and by the word of their testimony"* (Revelation 12:11).

Conquerors: *"In all these things we are **more than conquerors** through him that loved us"* (Romans 8:37).

Heirs: *"[We are] **heirs** of God, and **joint-heirs** with Christ"* (Romans 8:17).

Blessed: *"...who hath **blessed** us with all spiritual blessings in heavenly places in Christ"* (Ephesians 1:3).

2. We have what God says we have!

Life: *"He that hath the Son hath life; and he that hath not the Son of God hath not life"* (1 John 5:12).

Light: *"He that followeth me shall not walk in darkness, but shall have the light of life"* (John 8:12).

Liberty: *"Where the Spirit of the Lord is, there is liberty"* (2 Corinthians 3:17).

Love: *"The love of God is shed abroad in our hearts"* (Romans 5:5).

Joy: *"Your joy no man taketh from you"* (John 16:22).

Pardon: *"The blood of Jesus Christ...cleanseth us from all sin"* (1 John 1:7).

Peace: *"We have peace with God through our Lord Jesus Christ"* (Romans 5:1).

Purpose: *"For me to live is Christ"* (Philippians 1:21).

Power: *"Ye shall receive power, after that the Holy Ghost is come upon you"* (Acts 1:8).

Provision: *"My God shall supply all your need"* (Philippians 4:19).

Prospect: *"In my Father's house are many mansions.... I go to prepare a place for you"* (John 14:2).

3. We can do what God says we can do!

"I can do all things through Christ" (Philippians 4:13).

"In my name shall they cast out devils.... They shall lay hands on the sick, and they shall recover" (Mark 16:17–18).

We can share with the world what we have in Christ!

Affirm these words: "I am who God says I am. I have what God says I have. I can do what God says I can do."

35

RIGHT AND WRONG CONFESSIONS

E. W. KENYON

For a long time, I was confused over the fact that there was a continual sense of defeat and failure in my own life and the lives of others.

I prayed for the sick. I knew that the Bible was true, and I searched diligently to find the leakage. One day, I saw Hebrews 4:14 (ASV), which says that we are to *"hold fast our confession"* (*"profession"* in the Authorized Version).

Reading the third chapter of Hebrews, I discovered that Christianity could be called the "great confession."

+ I asked myself, "What confessions am I to hold fast?" I came up with these: I am to hold fast the confession of the absolute integrity of the Bible.

+ I am to hold fast the confession of the redemptive work of Christ.

+ I am to hold fast the confession of being a new creation, of receiving the life and nature of God.

- I am to hold fast the confession that God is the Strength of my life.

- I am to hold fast the confession that "surely He hath borne my sicknesses and carried my diseases, and that by His stripes I am healed." (See Isaiah 53:4–5.)

Though, I found it very difficult to hold fast the confession of perfect healing when I had pain in my body. I discovered that I had been making two confessions. I had been confessing the absolute truthfulness of the Word of God and, at the same time, making a confession that I was not healed.

If you had asked, "Do you believe that by His stripes, you are healed?" I would have said, "Yes, sir, I do." But in the next breath, I would have said, "But the pain is still there." The second confession would have nullified the first.

In reality, I'd had two confessions: first, a confession of my perfect healing and redemption in Christ, and second, a confession that the redemption and healing were not facts.

Then came the great battle to *gain* the mastery over my confession, until I'd learned to have but one confession. Now, if I confess, "My God shall supply every need of mine," I must not nullify that confession by saying, "Yes, God supplies my needs, but I cannot pay my rent. I cannot pay the telephone bill."

Faith holds fast the confession of the Word. Sense knowledge holds fast the confession of physical evidences. If I accept physical evidence over and against the Word of God, I nullify the Word, as far as I am concerned. But now I hold fast my confessions that God's Word is true; that by His stripes, I am healed; and that my God does supply my needs. I hold fast those confessions in the face of apparent contradictions, and God is bound to make good.

Many believers fail when things get difficult because they lose their confession. When the sun shines brightly, their confessions are vigorous, strong, and clear. But when the storms and testings come, and the adversary takes advantage of them, they give up their testimony.

Every time you confess disease and weakness and failure, you magnify the adversary above the Father and you destroy your own confidence in the Word. You are to hold fast to your confession in the face of apparent defeat. You are to study the Word until you know what your rights are, and then hold fast to them.

Some make confessions without any foundations. Then the adversary badly whips and beats them.

You are to find out what your rights are. For instance, you know that the Word says, "Surely He hath borne our sicknesses and carried our diseases." (See Isaiah 53:4.) So now you can make your confession. *"Nay, in all these things we are more than conquerors"* (Romans 8:37 ASV). There you can make your confession. *"Greater is he that is in you than he that is in the world"* (1 John 4:4 ASV). You can make your confession here.

Stand by your confession through thick and thin, through good report and evil. You know that your confession is according to the Word.

And they overcame him because of the blood of the Lamb, and because of the word of their testimony.

(Revelation 12:11 ASV)

36

NOT BORN TO BE DEFEATED

DON GOSSETT

First, when you were born again, you were not born to be defeated. You were born to be a conqueror. Declare it: "I am more than a conqueror through Christ!" (See Romans 8:37.)

Second, when the going gets tough, the tough get going. God says, "Arise, go over!" Don't sit there in defeat. Quit brooking in bewilderment. Shake off that feeling of frustration and arise, get going, for God is for you! Confess it: *"What shall we then say to these things? If God be for us, who can be against us?"* (Romans 8:31).

Third, here is how to triumph over that defeatist attitude: You have said, "I can't get my prayers answered"; now you say, "This is my *'confidence toward God…. Whatsoever* [I] *ask,* [I] *receive of him, because* [I] *keep his commandments, and do those things that are pleasing in his sight'* (1 John 3:21–22)." You have said, "I can't receive my healing"; now you say, "By His stripes, I am healed." (See Isaiah 53:5; 1 Peter 2:24.) You have said, "I can't see my loved ones saved"; now you say, "I believe for the saving of my household." (See Acts 16:31.)

Fourth, Joshua 1:2–9 is God's formula for victory and success. Our part is to *"arise, go over"* (Joshua 1:2), *"be strong and of a good courage*" (verse 6), "[be] *very courageous*" (verse 7), "*be not afraid, neither be thou dismayed*" (verse 9). And God's part is to be with us and to make us prosperous: "*I will be with thee: I will not fail thee, nor forsake thee.... For the* LORD *thy God is with thee whithersoever thou goest*" (verses 5, 9). The result: "*Then thou shalt make thy way prosperous, and then thou shalt have good success*" (verse 8).

Fifth, with God, nothing is hard. Jesus asked, "*Whether is easier*" (Matthew 9:5), not "Whether is harder," when He healed the palsied man.

Sixth, think victory, not defeat. Speak triumphant words, not defeat. Act like a conqueror, for in Christ, you are!

37

THE "UNSEEN YOU"

E. W. KENYON

Paul speaks of the hidden man of the heart. That is the *you* that is in you. The "visible you" is not the you that puts you over the top.

It is the "unseen you" who wins the fight.

The "seen you" may be very attractive or very repellent. It is the "unseen you" with whom we really wish to become acquainted.

It is the "unseen you," this hidden person of the heart, who runs the whole machinery.

This is the person who is to build you into a success.

This is the person who raises the money to put you over the top.

This is the one who made the "seen you" come across and make good.

It is the "unseen you" to whom I am writing this morning.

I am trying to cause this person to make the "seen you" study, work, and make yourself worthwhile in life's game.

It is the "unseen you" who makes the "seen you" worthwhile and makes you do things that have commercial value, who makes you do things that the world is waiting to have done.

I am saying to the unseen you, "Get behind this 'seen you.' Work. Study. Dig until you have won."

38

WHAT ARE YOU GOING TO DO?

E. W. KENYON

What of life? Perhaps you are standing on the threshold, getting ready to embark on untried paths. What are you going to do?

Have you chosen your work, vocation, and place in life, or are you drifting, hoping that something will turn up? It will, but the thing that will turn up will be of no value to you unless you are ready to take it as it comes.

Don't float. Dead fish float. Make up your mind that you will put your dreams into blueprints, and then, blueprints in hand, build your mansion.

In other words, find your place, but be sure that you do thorough preparatory work. Put real hard work into the days of preparation. Don't just get by. Don't be satisfied with anything but one hundred plus. Fight for it. Work for it. Enjoy it. Make it a game to win.

Be a success in youth, and you will be a success in middle life. You will be crowned in old age. And make yourself a wanted person. Be so valuable that if you had to move, men and women would weep because of your departure.

If you plan to be a minister, be God's best. If you go into business, be the best in your community. If you plan to be a lawyer or a physician, do it with a trained, cultured personality.

Whatever you do, plan to build your house on top of the hill. Harness that lazy mind and make it work. That mind can make a place for you.

Let me say to you, "Go under your own steam." Prepare yourself, and everywhere doors will open to you.

39

CAN IT BE GUARANTEED?

E. W. KENYON

Can everyone be successful?

I know that success belongs to every one of us, but the fear of failure hangs like a dark cloud over many lives. We may not be great financiers or great authors, but we may know that we have won in our place in life.

It is necessary that we make the right choice, find out what our talents and abilities are, and have them properly trained and fitted to achieve the desired end.

There are a few things that are absolutely imperative to fulfill our part of life's program. There must be a purpose from which we cannot be swerved. There must be the right kind of companionship. The wrong kind is a serious handicap, but it can be overcome. Some of us will be handicapped with physical environments that seem almost insuperable, but we can conquer.

A young man came to me just recently to talk over his future. He said, "So far, I have been a failure."

After he opened his heart to me, I saw where his difficulty lay. What he needed was God's help and companionship. I am not talking religion—for I never talk that—but this young man needed the help that only He, the great unseen One, can give.

He said, "Will you tell me just how to get in contact with God?"

He was genuine. That young man was real. My heart went out to him. There was something so big, so full of the right kind of ambition, that he challenged all that was in me.

I said to him, "It is necessary that you take Jesus Christ as your Savior and that you confess Him before your family, before the world, as your Lord."

He looked up at me and said, "That should not be difficult. No one should be ashamed of Him."

I said, "The moment you do it, God will give you eternal life. You will become His very own child. Then you will have not only the help of God as your own Father, but you will have the intercession and strength of Christ.

"Then He will give you the Holy Spirit, who will come into your life and live in you. You will soon find what this means. You can do a great deal alone, but when you have received eternal life within your spirit, your intellectual efficiency will increase 10 to 50 percent.

"As your mind is renewed through reading the Word, you will find a freshness in life such as you have never known. You will know that God is in you, that His ability is your ability.

"You can face any kind of a problem now and know that you are a victor. Your words will have something in them that they never had before. There will be a power in your very presence that men will feel.

"Always give God His place. Give Him a chance to show Himself. I don't mean that you are to talk religion to people. You just let God have His place in your life, and you will talk about Him.

"You will know that He is in you. You cannot fail with Him in you.

"'Nay in all these things, you are more than a success.' 'I can do all things through Him who gives me strength.' These mighty Scriptures will hold you. God will be the Strength of your life. He will make Jesus to be wisdom to you.

"That new, strange, wonderful, love nature of God will permeate your very being. You will be wanted. Men want genuine men and women around them. You will have the thing the world needs and the world lacks. You will find your place in life easily with this new addition of wisdom, strength, and ability in you."

You have read it. You have felt the thrill of new ambition tugging strongly at your heart.

Now, what are you going to do? Are you going to let it end with just a thrill, or are you going to begin now to make life worthwhile?

You have been stimulated. You have been lifted. Now go to work.

40

CONFESSION PRECEDES POSSESSION

DON GOSSETT

The following verses explain the way the faith system works:

With the mouth confession is made unto salvation.

(Romans 10:10)

We having the same spirit of faith, according as it is written, I believed, and therefore have I spoken; we also believe, and therefore speak. (2 Corinthians 4:13)

We confessed, and therefore we have salvation. Here are some other confessions that should characterize the life of Christians:

1. I confess that "God will save me, and I shall be a blessing." (See Zechariah 8:13.) I possess the ability to be a positive blessing, for by grace through faith, I am saved!

2. I confess that *"the LORD shall guide [me] continually"* (Isaiah 58:11). I possess the delight of a continually guided life.

3. I confess that "[God] *giveth his beloved sleep*" (Psalm 127:2). I possess refreshing, sound sleep.

4. I confess that "*the* LORD *shall preserve* [me] *from all evil*" (Psalm 121:7). I possess protection from all forms of evil.

5. I confess, "*Blessed be the Lord, who daily loadeth us with benefits*" (Psalm 68:19). I possess a life daily loaded with His benefits. (See Psalm 103:1–5.)

6. I confess, "*Acquaint now thyself with him, and be at peace: thereby good shall come unto thee*" (Job 22:21). I possess good things because I am acquainted with the Lord.

7. I confess that "*if any man serve me…him will my Father honour*" (John 12:26). I possess special honor from my Father, for gladly I serve Jesus.

8. I confess that "*he which soweth bountifully shall reap also bountifully*" (2 Corinthians 9:6). I possess bountiful financial blessings, for I am a generous, cheerful giver.

9. I confess, "*Can two walked together, except they be agreed?*" (Amos 3:3). I possess God walking with me, for I agree with Him by "speaking the Word," not my problems.

10. I confess that "[my name is] *written down in heaven*" (Luke 10:20). I possess a smile, my style, because my name is written down in the Lamb's Book of Life.

11. I confess that "my faith becomes effectual by acknowledging every good thing which is in me in Christ Jesus." (See Philemon 6.) I possess an effective faith life.

12. I confess "*the blessing of the* LORD, [that] *it maketh rich, and he addeth no sorrow with it*" (Proverbs 10:22). I possess wealth, and He adds no grief or pain with it.

13. I confess, "*Let the people praise thee, O God; let all the people praise thee. Then shall the earth yield her increase;*

and God, even our own God, shall bless us" (Psalm 67:5–6). I possess increase and abundant blessing because I daily praise the Lord.

14. I confess, *"Believe on the Lord Jesus Christ, and thou shalt be saved, and thy house"* (Acts 16:31). I possess the salvation of all my house; believers are receivers!

15. I confess that "[I] *have an unction from the Holy One, and* [I] *know all things"* (1 John 2:20). I possess this unction, which touches my service with the fragrance of heaven.

Remember, confession first, then possession.

41

PUTTING YOUR BEST
INTO WORDS

E. W. KENYON

Empty words hold no more interest than last year's bird's nest. When we are honest and fill our words with ourselves, our words will be honest. Others grow to depend on them.

I know a young man whose words are filled with love and unselfishness and a desire to help people. Whenever he speaks in the company of people, they listen to him.

Nowhere do words have as strange an effect as they do in a radio message. The minister who speaks over the air in a cold, dead voice will get a cold, dead response. No matter how beautiful the thoughts he has or how beautifully he clothes them, if his words are not filled with love and faith, they won't live.

Faith is built by words. Deeds have their place, but deeds are the children of words in large measure. You speak, then I watch you perform. It is your speech that attracts my attention. Your deeds have their place, and we give you credit for them, but it is your words that set us on fire.

You can fill your words with anything you wish. You can fill them with fear until the very air around you vibrates with doubt and fear and restlessness. You can fill your words with fear germs, and fill me with fear of disease and disaster.

Your words are either filled with interrogation points, with a sense of lack, with hunger and want, or you come to me and speak words filled with faith. Your faith words can stir me to the very depths. Then I wonder why I ever doubted. Your words enwrap me within themselves. They are like sunlight, warming a room on a cold, frosty day.

Your words can pick up my drooping, broken spirit and fill it with confidence to go out and fight again. Faith words are wonderful words.

The reason Jesus' words had such far-reaching influence was that they were faith words. When He said to the sea, *"Peace, be still"* (Mark 4:39), the very sea grew quiet, and the winds hushed their noise to hear the words of faith from the lips of the Man.

The deaf could hear His faith words. The lame and broken could rise and walk and run because of His faith words. There was something in His words that drove disease and pain out of the body and fear out of the heart.

I can hear John say, "I used exactly the same words as Jesus, but that boy was not healed. Now the Master takes the words out of my lips and fills them with something, and when they are heard, the child is healed." (See Matthew 17:16–21.)

What did Jesus put into His words that had such healing power?

A salesman was talking. He said, "I cannot understand it. I used the same argument, the same method, but I utterly failed.

"I used almost the identical words to talk to my client, and yet he said, 'No, I cannot buy today. I have no special interest in this thing.'

"Then the other salesman came and took my seat. He used the same formula that I had. The client became interested immediately. After a while, he reached into his pocket and pulled out his checkbook.

"What did that man have that I didn't?"

One man's words had been filled with pure mentality. He'd talked like a phonograph. The other had put living faith, interest, and love into his words. When the other salesman sat down, he'd had a look of quiet assurance on his face, and his first sentence had registered because he believed in the thing he was selling. He'd not only believed in it but believed that if the customer purchased it, it would be a blessing to him. It was a safe and wise investment.

This man had generated faith, created faith in the customer. The customer had put his hand in his pocket and held it there quite a while, holding on to his checkbook. By and by, he'd said, "I will take so many shares. That looks good to me."

His check had been written and signed. The deal had been made. Why? Because the salesman had filled his words with faith.

42

THE WRONG SLANT

E. W. KENYON

It is no use. I might as well give it up."

"Every time I try, I fail. Every job I get, I lose. Every dollar I get ahead—something happens and I have to use it. I am no further ahead now than I was ten years ago. There is something dead wrong somewhere."

I said to him, "Friend, what has been the difficulty?"

"I don't know."

I replied, "I will tell you what your trouble is, the way it appears to me—you have the wrong slant on life. You have talked about your failing, your difficulties, until they have become a mental disease.

"I venture to say that the last man you sought to find employment read you like a book and said, 'I don't want that man in my crew. He is a chronic fault finder.'

"You have had so much trouble that you have eaten it, slept with it, and dreamt it, until it had oozed out of you."

He said, "I know it, but how can I overcome it?"

"It is the easiest thing in the world to overcome. Solomon's solution was to *'trust in the LORD with all thine heart; and lean not unto thine own understanding'* (Proverbs 3:5). In other words, go into partnership with God, where you cannot fail."

"But that is religion."

"There is no religion about this. You are dead wrong. Religion is a man-made thing. This is a God-made thing. It is common sense to link up with God. You take Jesus Christ as your Savior, and you confess Him as your Lord. The moment you do, you receive God's life and ability, and you cannot fail. If you will walk with Him, you can no more fail than Jesus failed."

"But Jesus failed on the cross, didn't He?"

"Yes, but out of that failure came the greatest victory that the world has ever known. That was divine strategy. He will make you a conqueror if you walk with Him."

There are few who have walked with God and reached the top who have not been handicapped. Obstacles stand in the way of men who climb. I don't know why this is, but I know it is true. These obstacles have to be overcome, but in the overcoming, a person fits himself for places of responsibility.

I thank God for poverty, for need of self-denial, for self-culture, for long hours of study and hard work. The inward drive to plod on when tired is what makes men strong, self-reliant conquerors. Every failure stimulates them to work harder. There is no giving up. There is no yielding. Facing impossible circumstances becomes a daily experience to the conqueror.

He learns to win. He has cultivated the will to win, the will to conquer. He keeps the fires of ambition burning. He makes work a part of himself. He has a group of very fine habits. He has the habit of study, the habit of control of his eyes and ears, the control of his passions and ambitions.

He is master. He is the man who uses the public library and secondhand bookstores. He is ever studying to improve himself in his place. He knows his trade, his business, his profession. He makes himself an authority in his particular field. He counts his handicaps a blessing. He goes on with God and wins.

No man is a failure until he lies down and the undertaker puts him under the sod.

43

I AM STRONG

DON GOSSETT

Let the weak say, I am strong. (Joel 3:10)

Allow these following truths to strengthen your faith.

1. I am strong! This is the paradox of faith: I say I am strong when I am weak. This is faith's confession: I am strong.

2. No matter what I think of myself, I am strong. Regardless of others' opinions about my life, I am strong. When I feel the weakest, I am strong.

3. In spite of past experiences of succumbing to weakness, I rise up with a new testimony of faith: I am strong. It is not just when I feel strong that I say I am strong. But it is when I even feel weak that I declare I am strong.

4. God commands me to say that I am strong. This is saying what God says about my life. This is the language of faith. This is the language of victory.

5. What am I? I am strong. Whatever else I may be, I am strong. Wherever I am, I am strong.

6. What I confess, I possess. What I say is what I get. I confess, "I am strong" and I possess strength.

7. Why can I be so sure? In Joel 3:10 and countless other Scriptures, God declares that He is my Strength. So I gladly obey His command and say it, "I am strong." Never do I say, "I am weak." This would be disobedience to my God; it would grieve the Holy Spirit.

8. *"Let the weak say, I am strong"* (Joel 3:10).

44

HOW WE WIN

E. W. KENYON

Reason makes plans. The strong one—your will—carries them through. Dream, then carry out your dreams. Drive yourself to the finish line.

The will-less dreamer is never a success.

You have the vision. Make it come to pass. You dream your dream and then make the dream come true.

Cultivate a discontent with everything that is common in yourself. Compel yourself to improve your mind, your natural abilities. If you have the gift of cooking, be the best cook in the community. If you have a gift, no matter what it is, make that gift stand out until men admire it. Then someone will want to pay the price for it.

A young man had an unusual gift for dressing windows. He had worked in a store for a long time and had watched the window dresser and given him suggestions, until, by and by, the window dresser asked if he might become his helper.

It was but a few weeks until the helper became the artist. The head dresser never told his boss who did the artwork, but men came from different parts of the city to look at the windows. There was always a crowd in front of the store.

One day, a man came from a distance and asked who dressed the window, so the manager introduced him to the head dresser. The man was disappointed. He said, "He does not talk like one who could do this kind of work."

The young man stood by and later was introduced.

The man asked, "Do you dress these windows?"

And the young fellow replied, "I am only the sidekick."

"I have this amount of space in my window," the other said. "What would you do with it?"

The young man said, "If you will come back this afternoon, I will tell you."

He went into his office and drew the plans. When the man came back and looked at it, he said, "I will give you twenty-five hundred dollars a year if you go back with me."

He had been working for fifteen dollars a week.

You cannot hide trained genius. You cannot hide trained ability. Other people may use you for a time, but you will break the bonds sooner or later, as this young man did.

It is in you; pull it out.

45

GOD WILL WORK MIRACLES IN YOUR LIFE

DON GOSSETT

Expect a miracle every day. Be a miracle in your own life for the Lord. Here are nine reasons why you can expect God to work miracles for you:

1. *"If thou canst believe, all things are possible to him that believeth"* (Mark 9:23).

2. *"Verily, verily, I say unto you, He that believeth on me, the works that I do shall he do also; and greater works than these shall he do; because I go unto my Father"* (John 14:12).

3. *"Whatsoever ye shall ask in my name, that will I do, that the Father may be glorified in the Son"* (John 14:13).

4. *"If ye shall ask any thing in my name, I will do it"* (John 14:14).

5. *"Now unto him that is able to do exceeding abundantly above all that we ask or think, according to the power that worketh in us"* (Ephesians 3:20).

6. *"If ye have faith as a grain of mustard seed...nothing shall be impossible unto you"* (Matthew 17:20).

7. *"If two of you shall agree on earth as touching any thing that they shall ask, it shall be done for them of my Father which is in heaven"* (Matthew 18:19).

8. *"God hath set some in the church, first apostles, secondarily prophets, thirdly teachers, after that miracles, then gifts of healings, helps, governments, diversities of tongues"* (1 Corinthians 12:28).

9. *"To another the working of miracles; to another prophecy; to another discerning of spirits; to another divers kinds of tongues; to another the interpretation of tongues"* (1 Corinthians 12:10).

As you act upon these Scriptures, you can expect the Holy Spirit to minister miracles—miracles of healing, financial supply, intervention, deliverance, and salvation of souls. The Lord is ministering these truths to your heart, *"that he might make thee know that man doth not live by bread only, but by every word that proceedeth out of the mouth of the LORD doth man live"* (Deuteronomy 8:3).

46

LOOSE TALKING

E. W. KENYON

Careless speaking is a vicious habit. When one realizes that his words are the coin of his kingdom, and that his words can be a cursing influence or a blessing, he will learn to value the gift of speech. Control your tongue, or it will control you.

You will often hear men say, "I speak my mind." That is well if you have a good mind, but if your mind is poisoned, it is not good. An idle word spoken may fall into the soil of someone's heart and poison his whole life. What a blessing good conversation is and what a curse it's opposite. Make your tongue a blessing, never a curse.

A person is judged by his speech. Perhaps they never told you this, but people measure you by your words. Your words make you a blessing or a curse. Your words may carry a fortune in them. Learn to be the master of your conversation.

You are rated by your words. Your salary is gauged by the value of your words. Your words make a place for you in the business in which you are engaged. Neither jealousy nor fear can keep you from climbing to the top if your words have value that belongs at the top. The organization is bound to give you the place that belongs to you if your words bring forth the right results.

You don't have to put on. You don't have to exaggerate. All you have to do is be natural, but make that "natural" worth listening to.

Study your work. Study how to say things. Study how to use words that will change circumstances around you. Make a study, an analytical study of words, then see how much you can put into a single sentence. I don't mean how many words, but how much you can put into the words so that when men and women listen to your words, they will be thrilled by them.

The clerk in a five-and-ten store said "Good morning" in such a way that I turned to look at her. She had put something into her words. She had put herself, her personality, into her words. Her words rang.

She sold me some pencils at two for five cents, but she sold them as though she were selling a Pierce-Arrow car. After I had left the store, I felt inclined to go back and watch her deal with other customers.

Cut out the useless words that stand in the way. Eliminate all words that would hinder the thing you want to put over from reaching the mark. Make your words work in the hearts of those who listen. Trust in words—trust in the words of your own lips. Fill them with loving truth.

Think in your heart of how you want to help your customers, how you are going to bless them, and how the thing that you have is necessary to their enjoyment.

It is what you put into your words that makes them live in the hearts of the hearers. Empty words die in no-man's-land. They never get over the trench. If they do, they are duds. If they do get across and people hear them, they amount to nothing. On the other hand, living words—words bursting with heart messages— thrill and grip. Love always seeks the right word to convey its message so it is not lost in transit.

Clothe your thoughts in the most beautiful words, but don't sacrifice pungency for beauty. Blend them.

47

A BIG DEVIL AND A LITTLE GOD

DON GOSSETT

God is only as big as we allow Him to be in our lives. He will be to us what we believe Him to be. To most people, God is too small.

Perhaps you are one who has faith in a big devil and a little God, and your whole life reveals it. You have more faith in sickness than in health; more in weakness than in the Lord's strength; more faith in possessing fear than in God's gift of courage; more faith in lack than in God's supply of your needs; more faith in defeat and failure than in the triumphant life Christ gives. To give you the right faith, read 3 John. 2; Psalm 27:1; 2 Timothy 1:7; Philippians 4:19; and 2 Corinthians 2:14.

I challenge you to let God be big in your life. God is limited to the amount of your faith. He is "small" in the world as you make Him small. He is big only when you make Him big by using your divinely given authority.

It is important to have a scriptural appraisal of the devil and not one of your own making. Have a Biblesized God (and what a wonderful, big God the Bible reveals Him to be) and have a

Biblesized devil (and how the Bible limits his power toward the believer).

Both the saint and the sinner have troubles. The big difference is: *"The way of transgressors is hard"* (Proverbs 13:15) and *"many are the afflictions of the righteous: but the LORD delivereth him out of them all"* (Psalm 34:19). Both the saved and the unsaved have hard places, troubles and afflictions. But the unsaved have no deliverer; the righteous have a wonderful deliverer!

Affirm these truths: *"Greater is he that is in* [me], *than he that is in the world"* (1 John 4:4). *"Behold,* [God] *give*[s] *unto* [me] *power... over all the power of the enemy: and nothing shall by any means hurt* [me]*"* (Luke 10:19). *"In* [Jesus'] *name shall* [I] *cast out devils"* (Mark 16:17).

Don't allow Satan to "brainwash" you into believing in his subtle supremacy. He is a thief who comes *"to steal, and to kill, and to destroy,"* but Jesus has come that you *"might have life, and* [you] *might have it more abundantly"* (John 10:10). Believe in this big God of abundance—abundance of everything!

48

JESUS THE VICTOR

E. W. KENYON

We should fully understand this: No matter what a man's standing in heaven, if he has no faith, it does him no good. No matter what a man's privileges are, if the hand of faith is paralyzed, he cannot take hold of them.

As long as he is ruled by sin-consciousness, he has no sense of redemption. He is under condemnation, and Satan rules him. And as long as Satan rules, faith will be shriveled and undeveloped.

All through the Pauline revelation, from Romans through Hebrews, a complete redemption is taught. There is a perfect redemption. Satan is conquered.

> *Since then the children are sharers in flesh and blood, he also himself in like manner partook of the same; that through death he might bring to nought him that had the authority of death, that is, the devil.* (Hebrews 2:14 ASV)

Satan is stripped of his authority. Jesus triumphantly said, *"I am he that…was dead; and, behold, I am alive for evermore, amen; and have the keys of hell and of death"* (Revelation 1:18).

Satan was put to naught; his ability was paralyzed.

He put off from himself the principalities and powers, and made a show of them, openly triumphing over them in it.
(Colossians 2:15, Revised Version marginal reading)

Sin shall not have dominion over you.   (Romans 6:14)

Satan, then, has no dominion over us.

If redemption does not deliver us from sin-consciousness, it is no better than Judaism. If it cannot free us from condemnation, God and Christ have failed, and Satan has become the master. If sin-consciousness rules, acting on the Word is impossible. Where sin-consciousness rules, faith is a withered flower. The task of faith, then, is to get rid of sin-consciousness, and the Word is the only cure. It declares that we are redeemed.

In whom we have redemption through his blood, the forgiveness of sins.   (Ephesians 1:7)

If we have been redeemed, Satan's dominion is broken, and we are free. Not only has a perfect redemption been accomplished, but provision for a perfect recreation has been made.

Wherefore if any man is in Christ, he is a new creature: the old things are passed away; behold, they are become new. But all things are of God, who reconciled us to himself through Christ, and gave unto us the ministry of reconciliation.
(2 Corinthians 5:17–18 ASV)

There is a complete recreation and a complete reconciliation. If God has recreated us, we are not under bondage to the things of the old creation. If a man has been recreated, it is God's own work. He did it through the Holy Spirit and His own Word. So that new creation is effected by the impartation of God's own nature. We are actually born from above and become partakers of the divine nature. (See 2 Peter 1:4.) The old sin nature has gone, and a new nature, free from condemnation, has taken its place.

> *There is therefore now no condemnation to them that are in Christ Jesus.* (Romans 8:1 ASV)

> *Who shall lay anything to the charge of God's elect?... Who is he that condemneth?* (verses 33–34 ASV)

We have been made free from the law of sin and of death. God has justified us, or declared us righteous.

The word *justify* means to "make righteous." Righteousness is the ability to stand in the Father's presence without the sense of guilt, sin, or inferiority. We stand there as though sin had never been.

If redemption does not mean that, if the new creation does not give that, God has failed. The new creation must be as free from sin as Adam had been before he committed sin, or God has failed in His redemptive work.

Someone asks, "What about 1 John 1:6?"—"*If we say that we have fellowship with him and walk in the darkness, we lie, and do not the truth.*" He is speaking of broken fellowship. If a man says that he has fellowship with the Father when he is living under condemnation, he is telling a lie. Every man who is living in broken fellowship is walking in darkness. Likewise, if we say that we have not sinned when we are living out of fellowship, we are telling an untruth.

> *If we say that we have no sin, we deceive ourselves, and the truth is not in us.* (1 John 1:8 ASV)

However, if we acknowledge our sins and confess them, God is faithful to forgive us.

If we confess our sins, he is faithful and righteous to forgive us our sins, and to cleanse us from all unrighteousness.

(1 John 1:9 ASV)

If any man sin, we have an Advocate with the Father, Jesus Christ the righteous.   (1 John 2:1 ASV)

God not only makes us new creations; He makes us righteous.

That He might Himself be righteous and the righteousness of him that hath faith in Jesus.

(Romans 3:26 RV marginal reading)

This declares that He has become the righteousness of the man who has faith in Jesus as his Savior. If God has become our righteousness, we have a legal standing in His presence. First Corinthians 1:30 (ASV) tells us that He was made unto us righteousness.

But of him are ye in Christ Jesus, who was made unto us wisdom from God, and righteousness and sanctification, and redemption.

Then we have God as our righteousness and Jesus as our righteousness. A literal translation of Romans 4:25 would read, "He was delivered up on the account of our trespasses and was raised, because we stood righteous before Him."

Having been declared righteous, then, by faith, we have peace toward God through our Lord Jesus Christ.

(Romans 5:1 YLT)

Him who knew no sin [God] made to be sin on our behalf; that we might become the righteousness of God in him.

(2 Corinthians 5:21 ASV)

He not only becomes our righteousness, but now He also makes us His righteousness by a new birth, a recreation. We stand before Him reconciled, without condemnation, in fellowship with Him. If Scripture means anything, it means exactly what it says. The believer has a legal right to stand in the Father's presence without condemnation. (See Romans 8:1.) If He can do that, then acting on the Word is possible. And, if acting on the Word is possible, everything that belongs to us in Christ becomes available at once.

Victory over the enemy is one of the privileges of a son of God. When Jesus arose from the dead, He left an eternally defeated Satan behind Him. He is the Victor, so always think of Satan as the eternally defeated one.

49

VICTORY OVER THE ENEMY

DON GOSSETT

Here are some pointers on how to be successful:

Know your enemy. *"We are not ignorant of* [Satan's] *devices"* (2 Corinthians 2:11). Learn by the Spirit to discern the presence and work of evil spirits. (See 1 Corinthians 12:10.)

Know your rights. You are an overcomer of all Satan's work because of the blood of Jesus and the word of your testimony. (See Revelation 12:11.) Christ has given you power *and* authority over all the power of the devil. (See Luke 10:19.) Dare to use it.

Daily confess your stance in Christ. Your ground for sure victory is that Jesus defeated Satan, stripped him of his authority, and rose as the eternal Victor! With *"Christ in you,"* (Colossians 1:27), count heavily on this unshakeable fact: *"Greater is he that is in you, than he that is in the world"* (1 John 4:4). Daily make this your personal testimony!

Boldly quote the Word of God again Satan, as Jesus did. (See Matthew 4.) The Word is the Spirit's number one weapon when the enemy comes in like a flood. (See Isaiah 59:19.) Often quote the Word aloud to rout the enemy!

Free the captives. There are captives all around you that "ought to be loosed" (see Luke 13:16) from every bond of Satan. In the mighty name of Jesus, you can be God's instrument to liberate people from every kind of evil spirit.

Cast out evil spirits. Jesus said, *"In my name shall they cast out devils* [demons, evil spirits]" (Mark 16:17). Say, "In the name of Jesus, I command you evil spirits to depart." Stand your ground fearlessly, without wavering! Evil spirits know that they must submit to the name of Jesus! (See Philippians 2:9–11.)

Refuse to be Satan's "dumping ground," where evil spirits produce mental unsoundness; nervous disorders; spirits of gloom, heaviness, and depression; physical infirmities and diseases; and spiritual bondages. *"Resist the devil, and he will flee from you"* (James 4:7).

Plead the power of the blood of Jesus and live under the blood. Boldly speak God's Word against Satan. We are in a real warfare. (See Ephesians 6:12–16.) Casting out evil spirits is acting in the unseen "spirit realm," where we rely on the anointing of the Spirit as Jesus did. (See Luke 4:18; Acts 10:38.) Put on the whole armor of God. Wax bold against evil spirits in the name of Jesus. We are *"more than conquerors through* [Christ]" (Romans 8:37).

50

WHAT IS IN YOU?

E. W. KENYON

It is what you are, what you have in you, that counts. It is the undeveloped resources in your mind, in your spirit, in that inward man, that counts. It is the developing of a writer, a thinker, a teacher, an inventor, a leader, and/or a business manager that is hidden deep in you that is important.

I venture to say that every one of you young men and women who read this have one of these abilities. There may be an untrained voice or untrained musical abilities lying hidden under the careless, thoughtless exterior.

Let us go down with a flashlight and look over the untouched treasures that are stored away inside of you, which have never been touched, never been used. Then let us bring the thing up, that make it worthwhile, give it a commercial value. For, remember, everything that goes toward making you a success is inside of you. The thing that makes opportunities, makes money, saves money, creates new things, and brings together things that others have created but were unable to utilize, is inside of you. Find it and make it work.

This is going to require a boss who is utterly heartless to rule over you. The boss is inside of you. There is a slave driver in there, whom you must bring out. Put the whip in his hand, and tell him to go to it and make you a success.

There is something in you that can take these dreams of yours and make blueprints of them, and then can change the blueprints into buildings. That ability is there. No one else can train it. No one else can develop it. Someone else may set it on fire, but you can quench the fire by refusing to act.

Remember that you must use the suggestions that come; you must rise up and put the thing over. You must drive yourself, for no one else can do it.

Put yourself on a mental diet—not a diet of idle dreams or idle fancies but a diet of real mental work.

Be mentally awake, diligent. Put your best into every day. Make up your day of saved moments and hours.

You are out to win. You are out to conquer. You can do it. It would be different if this ability were in someone else, and you were trying to awaken it. But it is all in you, and you are going to put it over!

TRAIN YOURSELF

What you do for yourself counts far more than all that others have done or can do for you. Self-discipline is the most important feature in any life. Unless you put yourself under mental discipline, you will never develop the forces in you that are valuable to the commercial world.

Rule your temper so that no matter what happens, what is said or done, your temper will be under absolute control. The man who does not rule his temper can never achieve the success that belongs to him. He destroys the building that he erects. Govern your tongue, so that it will say nothing that injures anyone around you.

Practically all injury done to a business, home, or person is done with words. It is tongue work.

The man or woman who makes no contribution to destructive thought and talk is a valuable asset anywhere. He is deaf to anything that is destructive to another. He is blind to anything that folks do around him. He cannot speak of it. He has mastery of himself. The efficiency of an office force is reduced sometimes 50 percent by idle, unkind words.

The man who can govern his temper, his tongue, and his appetite, though he has but mediocre ability, is bound to get to the top. Gaining the mastery of these will be among his first real victories.

Controlled power is valuable. Waterfalls are simply beautiful, but they have no commercial value until they are harnessed. Likewise, it is the harnessed ability in you that is worthwhile, ability under intelligent mastery.

Find out what you wish to be or to do, then train yourself for it. What is undeveloped in you has no value. No one else either wishes or has the time to develop it. That is your business. The training is all done by you.

If you have a voice, put yourself under a teacher; then work and carry out the teacher's instructions. If it is art, put yourself under a competent instructor and obey the laws of art and work.

Nothing will take the place of hard work, intelligently directed. Talents in you need push and determination to make them worth money. It is you, and you alone, who will do the developing.

The lazy person who waits for something to turn up will be a failure. The only things that will turn up are rent and bills. Nothing will take the place of self-denial and hard work. It is easy to become a failure—all you need to do is idly dream.

It is the man who wills and keeps on willing who wins. Don't float. Don't wait for an opportunity. Go make your opportunity.

Put your whole self into life. Study; drive yourself. Always remember that your worst enemy is inside of you. No circumstance, no person, or combination of persons can conquer you as long as you do not destroy your own prospects.

Don't be satisfied with anything you do. Always seek to improve yourself.

ABOUT E. W. KENYON

Born in Saratoga County, New York, E. W. Kenyon (1867–1948) moved with his family to Amsterdam, New York, when he was in his teens. Kenyon studied at Amsterdam Academy, and, at the age of nineteen, preached his first sermon in the Methodist church there.

He worked his way through school, attending various schools in New Hampshire, as well as Emerson College of Oratory in Boston, Massachusetts.

Kenyon served as pastor of several churches in the New England states. At the age of thirty, he founded and became president of Bethel Bible Institute in Spencer, Massachusetts. (This school was later moved to Providence, Rhode Island, and is known as Providence Bible Institute.) Through his ministry at Bethel, hundreds of young men and women were trained and ordained for the ministry.

After traveling throughout the Northeast preaching the gospel and seeing the salvation and healing of thousands, Kenyon moved to California, where he continued his evangelistic travels. He was pastor of a church in Los Angeles for several years and was one of the pioneers of radio work on the Pacific Coast.

In 1931, he moved to the Northwest, and for many years his morning broadcast, *Kenyon's Church of the Air*, was an inspiration and blessing to thousands. He also founded the New Covenant Baptist Church in Seattle, where he pastored for many years.

During the busy years of his ministry, he found time to write and publish sixteen books, as well as many correspondence courses and tracts, and he composed hundreds of poems and songs. The work that he started has continued to bless untold thousands.

ABOUT DON GOSSETT

Don Gossett (1929–2014) served the Lord through full-time ministry for more than fifty years. Born again at the age of twelve, Don answered his call to the ministry just five years later and began by reaching out to his unsaved family members. Don apprenticed with many well-known evangelists, beginning with William Freeman, one of America's leading healing evangelists during the late 1940s. He also spent time with Raymond T. Richey, Jack Coe, and T. L. Osborn. Don's many writings have been translated into almost twenty languages and have exceeded twenty-five million in worldwide distribution. His daily radio show, launched in 1961, has been broadcast worldwide. Don raised five children with his first wife, Joyce, who died in 1991. In 1995, Don found lifelong love again and married Debra, an anointed teacher of the Word. They ministered worldwide and lived in British Columbia, Canada, and in Blaine, Washington State.